PROGRESSIVE
FLYING

PROGRESSIVE FLYING

Developing
Skills And
Using Your
Private Pilot's
Licence

JAMES ALLAN

Airlife
England

Copyright © 1997 James Allan

First published in the UK in 1997
by Airlife Publishing Ltd

British Library Cataloguing-in Publication Data
A catalogue record for this book
is available from the British Library

ISBN 1 85310 819 7

Typeset by Phoenix Typesetting, Ilkley, West Yorkshire.
Printed in England by Livesey Ltd, Shrewsbury.

Airlife Publishing Ltd
101 Longden Road, Shrewsbury, SY3 9EB, England.

CONTENTS

INTRODUCTION

When you first got your Private Pilot's Licence (PPL) from the United Kingdom Civil Aviation Authority (CAA) you probably thought that it was rather a disappointing looking document, just a slip of buff-coloured paper. But that flimsy brown certificate does represent something of real significance. It marks the culmination of your basic flying training, though not by any means the end of your learning how to fly. It is the one tangible reward you get for a great deal of study, a certain amount of sacrifice, considerable mental and physical effort and a far from negligible financial investment. You have spent a lot of your time studying text books, travelling to the aerodrome (sometimes only to hang around there in less than ideal training weather, waiting hopefully to fly), occasionally actually doing some flying, being debriefed and travelling home again. The money you have spent to get this little bit of paper could have bought you the holiday of a lifetime perhaps, QE2 to NY and then back in Concorde. Alternatively it could have been turned into a deluxe fitted kitchen, or it might have enabled you to buy a turbo-GTI car, complete with CD player and quadraphonic hi-fi, to replace the tired old vehicle you are still running.

Instead you have acquired this little bit of buff-coloured paper? So what are you going to do with it now you have it? You can (like rather too many other people who get their PPLs) brag about your achievement and do little more than bask in the reflected glory of being a qualified pilot. You can perhaps be a little more daring and make one or two Sunday afternoon trips to a neighbouring airfield and have a coffee and sandwich there before flying home again. But you will soon realise that, at real costs amounting to around £30 for a coffee and £40 for a sandwich, this isn't actually the most economical way of quelling your thirst or pangs of hunger. You will almost certainly take some of your friends on flights that are little more than extended circuits around the airfield.

Eventually you are bound to wonder why on earth you were so stupid as to spend all that time and money on learning to fly. It is a dreadful shame how many newly qualified private pilots do have periods when they think that like this. It is all the more mortifying because your PPL can open up some marvellously enjoyable opportunities for you. If you are looking for some ideas, read on a little and I hope you will soon discover enough about some of these opportunities to help you to adopt a much more positive attitude about your future as a pilot.

Danger to Avoid

The greatest danger that lies in wait for most private pilots is not engine failure, fire in the air, flight into bad weather or any of the other emergencies your instructor has just finished teaching you to cope with; it is boredom. Since it would be bad for business to tell you about it, I bet neither your instructor nor the management of your flying club or school were ever kind enough to warn you about this boredom. It is in fact one of the best kept secrets in the flying training world. But it is true. After the first flush of excitement and enthusiasm it is all too easy to find the local scenery from the air getting boring; flying solo (because you have run out of friends to take flying) gets boring too; the snacks in the 'greasy spoons' of the few easily accessible local airfields soon begin to taste even more boring; the sluggish Cessna with its draggy legs sticking out in the slipstream becomes a boring machine to fly; flying itself can be a pretty damn boring business because (thankfully) emergencies never seem to occur and you don't now have an instructor sitting there beside you ready to spring nasty surprises on you. Flying seems to have lost its challenge, and with it, its fun. But things really don't have to get like that. Honestly!

Making it all Worthwhile

Instead of getting into such a frame of mind you can go on to turn your PPL into one of the most rewarding investments you have ever made. That is what this book is all about. It is for the pilot whose logbook is beginning to show longer and longer gaps between the flights it records, or where the 'From' and 'To' columns are gradually being filled up with ditto marks. It is for the owner who finds dandelions and long grass have grown tall enough to hide the main wheels each time he or she returns to the aircraft. It is for the pilot whose left shoe soles wear out before the right ones and whose rudder leans permanently to the left from constantly flying boring circuits and bumps. It is for the pilot who is beginning to feel a bit like a tennis ball, always flying to and fro along the same unadventurous route between the same two familiar airfields.

One way of making worthwhile use of your PPL is to use it as your first step towards a Commercial Pilot's Licence (CPL) and then possibly an Airline Transport Pilot's Licence (ATPL). That way, the dividend on your PPL investment could be nothing less than your future career earnings. But that is *not* what this book is about. It is really written for the airmen and airwomen who earn their living outside commercial piloting but who are keen enough about flying for their interest to carry them through to the successful completion of a PPL course. It is written mainly for the private pilot, young in either years or flying hours, but it is also for any pilot who, regardless of age or experience, has begun to wonder 'Where does my flying go from here? What can I do with my PPL now?'

These questions have come into almost every pilot's mind from time to time. Sometimes a spell of bad weather brings this feeling on; occasionally a personal cash crisis. It hits others shortly after they've completed an advanced rating (multi-engine or instrument flying perhaps) and they wonder then what to do next. But many pilots are liable to find these feelings of doubt creeping into their minds quite soon after they get their new PPLs. They no longer have an instructor to shepherd them along; to encourage them to go that one stage further; to plan for them what they are going to do with each new hour in the air. For the first time in their flying lives they have to set their own objectives, decide their own destiny.

If you are one of these pilots, and if you are also a prudent pilot, you will soon begin to realise that completion of your PPL course hasn't magically turned you into a pilot for all seasons and all ventures. You may very well feel you have finished learning to fly. What you may still have to realise is that your PPL is really not much more than a licence allowing you to start learning about flying. And no good pilots ever come to the end of that stage of their education.

The aim of this book is to help you really enjoy using the privileges of your PPL by constantly extending your knowledge of flying. It is not in any way an attempt to encourage you to take stupid risks; quite the contrary in fact. But it does try to help you put into a sensible perspective some of the more alarming aspects of flying that often seem to take an altogether too prominent place in training syllabuses. You have been brought up on a diet of engine failure procedures and forced landings. The awesome power of a thunderstorm has been dinned into you over and over again. The thought of seeing ice build up on the wings of your aircraft almost certainly causes shivers to run up and down your spine. Learning how best to handle (or even better, how to avoid) situations like these has a very proper place in all safety-conscious flying training, but these skeletons must never be permitted to cast their long shadows across the rest of your flying life. You have got to remain ever alert to the dangers associated with these aspects of flying and you must keep yourself prepared and in good practice to cope safely with them. However, as you will discover in later chapters of this book, there is a great deal more to enjoying the privileges of being a pilot than sitting on the edge of your left-hand seat, nervously waiting for the next emergency to strike.

You will also learn here something about how to cope with weather you never met whilst training and how best to avoid the types of weather you are really better never to tangle with. You will find out the advantages and drawbacks of various types of aircraft, what they can do for you and what you can do with them. You will be encouraged to develop new skills: night flying; instrument flying; aerobatics; precision flying. If your basic training was done at a big commercial airport, you will learn how to fly safely in and out of little grass strips; if you did most of your flying training at one of these smaller, quieter aerodromes, isn't it high time you learned how to mingle competently and confidently with the airliner traffic at major airports? You will get to know and recognise your own limitations and develop the judgement and airmanship that will ensure you fly safely within these limitations.

Follow some of the suggestions here and perhaps one of these days you will find yourself having the wonderful experience of introducing your own grandchildren to the joys of flying in little aeroplanes. In this way too, you should also become and stay a safe enough pilot to go on year after year enjoying all the many other pleasures and the thrills, as well as the enormous satisfaction that a private pilot's licence can bring into your life.

Chapter 1

Taking Care of Your Passengers

Your First Fellow Travellers

Even before you started learning to fly you probably already had a mental list drawn up of the friends you were going to take flying as soon as you got your licence. There were your girl/boyfriend, fiancé(e) or spouse, brothers and sisters, parents, children perhaps, workmates and neighbours. In one way you were perhaps rather hoping to impress them and in another way you were simply wanting to share with them something of your new-found pleasure in being a pilot. As soon as you have your PPL in your hand, you are legally entitled to be the captain of a passenger carrying aircraft, provided of course that particular aircraft is included in the privileges of your licence. You are also entitled to defray some of the costs of your flying (as explained in more detail in Chapter 5) by sharing expenses with your passengers. It probably won't be very long after your PPL arrives when you coax the first unsuspecting soul into the aircraft with you. Just make sure you both enjoy the experience!

Many pilots annotate their logbooks with the names of the folk who have flown with them, occasionally totting them all up and claiming they have now flown more than such-and-such a number of passengers. A more important total, I often feel, would be the number of people who have entrusted their lives to you in the air on more than one occasion.

Attune yourself to your Passenger

When you are taking someone up for a flight it is particularly important that you attune yourself to your passenger's feelings. You have your piloting job to do, but spare an odd moment away from the vigilant look out, the careful scanning of the instruments and all your other duties of airmanship, to sneak an occasional glance at your companion in the cockpit. If your passenger is grinning like a

11

Cheshire cat, all is probably going well. The whole idea of the flight is for you both to have a good time. If there is a somewhat anxious or puzzled look on the face beside you, try to find out why and do your best to give the necessary reassurances or answers. If there is a chalky pallor accompanied by deep breathing, locate a sick bag and head straight for home. Nobody is going to enjoy a flight under these circumstances. Being sensitive to your passenger's feelings is so much easier now that side by side cockpit seating is the norm for most aeroplanes. I vividly remember one of my early passengers, a girlfriend I was taking up in a Tiger Moth on her very first flight. An aeroplane with tandem open cockpits, where the passenger sits up in front of you, makes it tricky to see facial expressions! Having to communicate with each other by shouting through a rubber tube with a mouthpiece didn't help much either. Just about ten minutes into the flight I saw her leather-gauntletted hand jabbing vigorously towards the ground below and heard her shouting what sounded like 'I want back down' as she gesticulated. I made a gentle Rate 1 turn back towards the airfield and within a very few minutes the Tiger's wheels were rumbling over the grass again. However fond I was of the girl (and I have to admit I really did like her) I felt very glad we had made it back down safely before any vomit had sprayed back in the slipstream. That sort of thing can put a strain on any friendship. Unfortunately, as soon as I shut the engine down I found myself on the receiving end of a tirade from a very disappointed and not in the least unwell young lady. 'That was one hell of a short flight! Why on earth did you turn back like that?' I explained what a considerate pilot I thought I had been; then she made it abundantly clear to me that she had not been feeling in the slightest airsick and had merely been trying to ask me 'What's that town?' Nice girl she was too; never did see much of her after that. That was my first lesson on how very important it can be to keep alert as to how your passengers really are feeling about the flight.

Thoughtfulness for First-Timers

Almost a century after man made his first powered flight, over three-quarters of the British population have still never been in the air. Of those who have flown, the vast majority know flying only from the point of view of a passenger in a large commercial aircraft. So, even though the environment of a little single piston engine aeroplane may have become second nature to you now, don't forget it is probably totally new and very strange to your passengers. You owe it to them to explain things in advance. The cockpit may look quite like the inside of a car but tell them that once the engine starts it is going to be a great deal noisier than inside a Toyota or a Volkswagen. Front seat passengers must be made well aware that their hands and feet should stay clear of the controls throughout the flight and they should be warned not to distract you at critical times like take-off and landing. Instruments look interesting to some passengers; tell them a little about what the more easily understood ones are for. Don't bore others about the panel, knobs and switches if they show no curiosity about them. They'll get more enjoyment from looking out of the windows. Small aeroplanes often bank more steeply than airliners so explain that, even if the wing on their side suddenly appears to have vanished, they are in no danger of falling out. Unexpected noises can cause alarm. If the aircraft you are flying has a stall-warning klaxon or bell, your passengers will appreciate knowing about it before it blasts off in their ears, perhaps sounding to them like a heavy truck trying to overtake just as you cross the threshold to land. Unexpected silences can frighten people too. Let your passengers know in advance that it is quite normal for things to go a bit peaceful as you throttle back to descend or land.

Comfort Factors

Tell your passengers, before you go out to the aircraft, that there is no toilet on board. This is probably the first aircraft they have encountered that doesn't have that important accessory fitted as standard. Show where the sick bags are stowed, just in case someone should 'feel unwell'. (It is best to avoid using the actual word 'sick'.) It is best also to avoid using lots of technical words you may well be familiar with but which are likely to be just jargon to your passenger. Trailing edge, walkway, aileron, bank, backtrack are just some of these. Most non-flyers think that 'stall' means the engine abruptly stopping, as in the case of a car engine, while the terms 'sideslipping' and 'skidding' can also be alarming concepts to someone more used to driving than flying.

Unless it is a fry-eggs-on-the-concrete day, close all doors and windows before taxying out; it makes inexperienced passengers feel very insecure to have open gaps and draughts once you are on the move. Taxi slowly and try not to jerk passengers with sudden jabs of brake or abrupt turns. Remember that ATC radio chat is incomprehensible to most non-flyers. It is worth giving your fellow travellers some idea of what this gibberish is all about. Just imagine what the effect on a first-time passenger might be on hearing what sounds like 'Deceiving your stench live; queuing ache diner-hate-tree; Runaway induce two sick; Queer taxi to hold a pint whisky.' And that's just before you take-off! What about a slightly anxious passenger overhearing a reassuring transmission while up in the air apparently along the lines of 'Kill a Yankee's cock one for sex heaven with high dent' or some similarly baffling gobbledygook? (That call might also remind you to explain why there is a green light flickering erratically on the instrument panel too. Occasionally passengers who spot the transponder light get the disquieting feeling that it must be trying to draw the pilot's attention to something that's going horribly wrong.)

If your passenger has never been up in a small plane before, try to pick a nice clear day and a quiet still air time for the flight. Air turbulence and gusty conditions play havoc with sensitive stomachs and peering into haze isn't going to impress many passengers with the joys of aviating in little aeroplanes. This is no time either for you to try to show your skills as a potential aerobatic ace or combat pilot. Keep the turns gentle, climb and descend only at reasonable angles. Try to explain manoeuvres in advance and you will find passengers much less likely to jump and clutch at the coaming, door handle, controls or your elbow each time the engine note changes or the aircraft banks. Above all, do your best to pull off a greaser when the flight is coming to an end. Passengers all talk to their friends about their experience and what they thought of their pilot's proficiency. It may not have seemed a bad bounce from your point of view but with nothing to compare it with, the passenger could well have a very different opinion of your landing. Just think what you would feel about the driving skill of someone who thumped the front bumper of the car into the house wall as you came back from a trip together. It is worth it, for your own esteem if for no other reason, to get good at making smooth landings and then practice staying that way!

Experience and Safety

You might find some of your friends are a little reluctant to fly with you too soon after you qualify for your PPL. Understandably (and as it happens quite correctly) they feel you are somewhat lacking in experience compared with an ATPL qualified pilot, and so they may not yet be inclined to risk their necks with you at the controls. You could try explaining that statistically one of the safest periods in a pilot's career covers the first few dozen flying hours after getting a PPL. You have all the training fresh in your mind and, still being a little unsure of yourself, you are more likely now than later to ask advice about anything unusual, check the weather carefully, preflight the aircraft meticulously. It is a sad fact that, if you are like many pilots, by the time you have about 200 hours logged you'll begin to feel you know it all and, believing you've got enough experience now, think you can dispense with some of these 'student pilot' attitudes. The accident charts show the sad result of this. And, assuming (like the vast majority of pilots) you make it safely through that 200–hour phase, it is worth remembering there is another significant blip in the accident charts for pilots with just about 1000 hours under their belts.

Briefing is Obligatory

You may feel that giving so much information to a passenger who is just going up with you for something as simple as an extended circuit of the airfield, really is going a bit over the top. It isn't. Under the law, the commander of any UK registered aircraft (whether it is a balloon, microlight, helicopter, light aircraft or airliner) is required to ensure that a suitable briefing is given to all passengers on board. Obviously, there is no need to explain regulations about not carrying explosives, acids and compressed gasses if no luggage is involved, and how to cope with a ditching is somewhat superfluous for a 20 minute local flight around an inland airfield. But you are legally obliged to warn all passengers of the dangers of propellers, explain how to operate the safety harness, door locks, catches and exits from the aircraft (including kicking out a window should the plane overturn after a forced landing). You must explain how best they should brace them-selves before any forced landing and show them where to find the fire extinguisher and first-aid kit, if any.

It is not obligatory (but often makes passengers feel they are more like part of the crew and less like useless pieces of self-loading cargo) if you explain the importance of maintaining a good look out and ask them to help by pointing out any other aircraft they see (high-flying jets excepted). An extra pair of eyes to cover your blind spots never comes amiss, especially when in and around a busy circuit, and the average passenger is delighted to feel useful during the flight.

Spreading the Gospel

The last thing you want to do when flying passengers is to put them off the whole idea of flying in light aircraft. Treating the flight as being primarily for their benefit and not purely for your own will certainly help prevent that happening. Once you find that the passengers you fly are really enjoying being up with you (and not just saying they do, to make you feel better) you could think about extending the range of people you carry. You will, after all, eventually run out of friends and relations, even if some do agree to fly with you more than once.

General Aviation (GA) will flourish in the future only if a regular supply of new student pilots show up to learn and only if GA's often ill-informed opposition lobby can be successfully fended off. As a good private pilot you can play your part in both of these areas. By taking along as a passenger (perhaps on a flight you were going to make anyway) some air-minded youngster you know, you may be helping to produce the next generation of student pilots. The American Experimental Aircraft Association (EAA) runs a scheme called the 'Young Eagles', under which private pilots volunteer to give short air-experience flights to children between 8 and 17 years of age. In the UK this excellent idea is operated under the auspices of the Popular Flying Association (PFA) and by participating in this you could be helping in both ways. Some of the children you fly may well end up becoming pilots themselves as a result of the seed you have helped to sow. Others may become local councillors, politicians or MPs who, as a result of learning at least a little about flying will be more likely to look upon light aviation from a more favourable point of view. They could approve, instead of oppose, a planning application for an airfield, or maybe even ensure that the interests of GA are not forgotten in some future transportation white paper.

Message for the Media

You might also like to consider flying yet another category of passenger. General Aviation, and light aircraft in particular, tend to get a pretty raw deal from the media. A lot of the inaccurate news coverage that you read is not so much biassed as simply uninformed. By writing and reporting like this, news reporters and journalists tend to adversely affect the general public's whole idea of light aviation, simply because they misunderstand the subject. One quick trip in a Cessna isn't going to give any journalist a thorough education on how to write about aviation themes in future, but it can go a long way towards preventing him or her going into print with a half-baked report maligning small aeroplanes, before first checking on the facts.

If you know a television, press or radio reporter, why not consider inviting him or her to come along with you for a flight? Make sure the aeroplane is looking its neat and tidy best, pick the right weather, resist the temptation to throw the aeroplane about the skies. Do all you can to give this important passenger as good a first impression of GA as you can. By doing something along these lines you can certainly help dispel, in at least that member of the media, some of the frequent misconceptions that exist about light aviation. You'll then have done your bit to ensure that your latest passenger's reports will be more factual in future, and less biassed against small aircraft.

Faint-hearted Flyers

Flying is not a natural part of human life in the way that it is inherent in the lives of most birds, give or take the odd kiwi or penguin. Even in advanced countries like the USA, the UK and other European states, which are constantly being flown over by scheduled services and holiday charter airlines, significant numbers of the population have never left the ground. Many of these people have just never had any occasion to take to the air, but many others have never flown because of anxiety or even downright fear of flying. Some research carried out by the University of Bristol has shown that between 20% to 25% of individuals in Western populations are apprehensive about flying, even in airliners, never mind small two-seat or four-seat light aircraft. In 1989, Norwegian researchers established that, of the people who actually do fly in commercial airliners some 21% of female passengers are always afraid of flying. The Boeing company has also gone into this field of research and has concluded that about 17% of the US population is afraid of flying and 24% of all airline travellers experience some feelings of anxiety. (They reckon that their customers, the airlines, are losing several millions of dollars of revenue every year because many of the 17% of people who are afraid of flying make a point of avoiding the experience altogether.)

Given this background, it is virtually certain that some of the people you fondly imagine would be delighted to have you offer to take them flying, will instead be scared stiff at the very idea of going up with you. Don't take it too personally. It is very likely to be because your potential passenger believes that if man had been intended to fly, God would have given him wings. Many people also suffer to some degree from what could clinically be termed a phobia about flying, an irrational, exaggerated fear that is totally out of proportion to the level of danger actually involved. Despite being quite comfortable yourself, sitting in a small, lightly constructed machine supported several thousand feet above the ground in thin air, you perhaps have some phobias of your own. How do you fancy tightrope walking (without a safety net, of course)? Or an afternoon potholing deep down under the Mendips, perhaps? You might on the other hand prefer dangling at the end of a nylon rope off some vertical cliff-face in the Cuillins of Skye? A weekend adventure camping among the snakes (or spiders) in a jungle clearing then? Or maybe a month long underwater cruise in one of the Royal Navy's Trident submarines? Most of us have some hang-ups of our own, so you should never deride a panic-stricken passenger. Whatever you do, don't try too hard to cajole him or her into flying with you. You both might regret it in the end.

Partner Problems

When the un-air-minded person involved happens to be the pilot's partner, the situation can be particularly serious. However enthusiastic newly qualified pilots may be, however determined to make full use of their PPLs, the fact that their husbands, wives or other close partners constantly refuse to fly with them often makes it only a matter of time before that nice new hard-earned PPL ends up lying forlornly in the back of a desk drawer. Then the closest its owner is ever likely to come to piloting again is longingly casting a wistful look at cruising Katanas and passing Pipers. What a waste of a good licence; what a downright shame it is when that sort of thing happens.

Popular Misconceptions

Fear of flying is largely groundless. Statistically, flying is safe. Airliners are safer than little aeroplanes admittedly, but even light aircraft have a pretty good safety record. One of the troubles here is that flying tends to get a bad press. Headlines in the media about air show fatalities greatly outnumber reports of the far more numerous air shows that take place, devoid of any mishap. Typical sensational local newspaper stories of perhaps an injury free misjudged landing seldom make mention of the fact that this 'accident' was the first incident of its kind to take place at the local aerodrome for many years. To many non-flyers, the mental image of a pilot is a young, physically fit male, possessed of a reckless brand of macho courage and with little sense of danger. (World War 2 flying films have a lot to answer for). Not feeling themselves to be in that category, the reluctant passengers simply opt out of anything to do with small aeroplanes.

Luckily, this irrational fear is not insuperable. Many competent pilots made their first flights with distinctly sweaty palms and dryness of the mouth, yet soon got over that and went on to learn to enjoy flying thoroughly. There is an ancient Chinese belief that to conquer a beast you must first find it beautiful, and there is no doubt that once a person begins to discover the real beauty of flight, then flying ceases to hold the terror it may once have done. Psychologists tell us that not many people are really scared of anything they fully understand. To the lay person, quite how a lump of metal (or plastic or wood) with human beings inside it gets itself up into thin air and, what is more, actually manages to stay up there unsupported, remains an incomprehensible mystery. Clear up at least some of that mystery and in many cases you automatically clear up a lot of the anxiety as well. Simple explanations in advance, of what is likely to happen, do usually help to calm nervous passengers in the air too. The facts that engines are noisy on take-off and that banking to turn is standard practice should be spelled out. Passengers should also be made aware that thermals and turbulence tend to affect light aircraft more than they affect airliners and that the odd bump or lurch doesn't herald the end of life as we know it.

Popular misconceptions abound concerning light aircraft. Many non-flyers believe it to be a fact that they inevitably drop out of the sky if they are so unfortunate as to fly into one of these mysterious phenomena known as 'air-pockets.' All your passengers who drive know that if you stall the engine of a car you are left powerless and helpless unless you can get it started again. They have heard that light aircraft can stall too and naturally presume that this is liable to have similar, but even more disastrous, results. A simple clarification of some such facts of flying (though not an erudite aerodynamic explanation) can go a long way towards calming unfounded fears. Some people are scared silly about making fools of themselves by being airsick. Often the very fact that they are anxious can aggravate this situation. Even as simple a matter as knowing that there are sick bags easily accessible can reduce tension and make an apprehensive passenger immediately feel better about this. So too can a pilot who is determined to fly smoothly (avoiding steep banks and being gentle whenever changing from climbing to level flight), who tries to keep the passenger interested in what is going on and never attempts to show off his or her skills as an airman (other than by pulling off a greaser of a landing). You may have your own ideas about which phase of flight is the most hazardous but nothing will ever convince Joe or Jill Public that anything is more dangerous than the landing. To them that is a well-known scientific fact. Expect a slight frisson from your passengers as you near that stage of the flight and do your best, when you have any inexperienced passengers on board, to make your landing an especially smooth one.

Reassuring the Anxious

The Bristol University study mentioned earlier, asked a random selection of passengers who were waiting for flights in the Gatwick departure lounge, what aspects of flying they were most anxious about. The 'unnaturalness of flying' and 'fear of falling out of the sky' were equal first. Following these, in order, came 'loss of personal control over the situation', 'take-off', 'landing' and 'instability of the aeroplane'. Among a group of people attending a course specifically designed to help them overcome fear of flying, the main anxiety arousers were similar, together with 'fear of the unknown'. Very few people, according to this study, are unduly worried about mechanical or technical failure of the engine or aircraft. Just the same it does no harm to take any obviously nervous passenger with you as you collect and study the Met forecast, so demonstrating that you also take that aspect of safety seriously. Explain why you are, or are not, filing a flight plan. This is because many people seem to regard flying without filing a flight plan as hazardous in the extreme, one result of frequent newspaper reports of aircraft accidents which include the ostensibly critical remark that 'the pilot had not filed a flight plan'. As you do the preflight walk round, explain what you are doing and perhaps contrast this prudent procedure with the average car driver who is quite happy to launch into a high-speed motorway journey without so much as an oil level or tyre pressure check. It is probably also worth mentioning that all aircraft have mandatory servicing, and that components like the engine and instruments are 'lifed' unlike a private car which is all too often simply driven to the stage where the AA have to be called to tow it home. Point out that light aircraft have two ignition systems, two sets of spark plugs and (if appropriate) two VHF radios, two fuel pumps, two fuel tanks etc, to provide back up in the unlikely event of any of these happening to fail.

When mentioning the dreaded 'failure' word, you should also mention that even if the engine were to fail up there, this would not mean the whole contraption hurtling down to an inevitable crash in the way many non-flyers imagine it would. Explain how well a light aircraft can glide and how the one you are flying can, if necessary, be landed safely in almost any reasonably sized agricultural field. Offer to demonstrate what happens if you pull the power off in flight . . . but never force that demonstration on a reluctant passenger. That might make matters worse instead of better.

Stopping Spouses Shivering

For the really reluctant spouse or partner, one of the courses run to help people cope with flying fears is probably worth considering. These are designed primarily for airline passengers but most of them do cover a lot of ground relevant to all flying. 'Fear of Flying' courses are run every few weeks at London (Heathrow) and Manchester International Airports by Aviatours (Charter) Limited. Each lasts for one day, during which participants are given a talk by an experienced airline captain on popular misconceptions about flying, how aircraft stay in the air, why they bank when they turn and what all these odd noise level changes mean. He is also happy to answer questions on topics that seem to worry potential passengers, such as what happens if the plane gets hit by lightning, or an engine fails, or the undercarriage sticks in the up position. After lunch the course is taken over by a psychologist who explains how panic attacks can be coped with, explains that flying phobia, whether genetic or acquired, can be conquered and gradually prepares the students on the course for its third and decisive phase. This is where they are invited to board a Boeing aircraft for a flight to see how they feel about flying after their new insight into what flying is all about. Occasionally some participants fall at this last hurdle and won't leave the departure lounge, but the majority screw up enough courage to make the 45 minute flight. During it, the captain explains everything that is going on in a running commentary on each move, bump, whine, change in attitude or noise level. Passengers who previously were panic stricken have been known to come down after these flights having paid a visit to the flight-deck, marvelled at the panorama below them and thoroughly enjoyed the experience. For others the course was of more limited success, but many who previously were nervous wrecks at the very thought of getting into an aeroplane, have become much more relaxed about the whole business of flying. A course of this nature costs no more than a couple of hours rental of a club aircraft; if it could turn a reluctant spouse into a willing passenger that could be money very well spent.

As an alternative, or as a follow-up, what the Americans call a 'Pinch-hitter' course might also make a good investment. These short courses are designed, not to teach non-flyers to become qualified pilots, but to take them to the stage where they would be perfectly capable of getting a light aircraft safely back onto the ground if the pilot were to be incapacitated in flight. And believe it or not, that remote possibility is a source of more refusals to fly in small aeroplanes than you might imagine. No-one wants their partner to collapse with a heart attack at any time, but the idea of this happening while your partner is up in an aeroplane that you are piloting, can be a pretty terrifying thought. It is not difficult to understand this attitude of mind either. Just imagine how you would feel, abandoned aloft in an aeroplane, not knowing anything at all about how to work that mysterious VHF radio, not having a clue about how to get the aircraft back down onto the ground again, and beginning to see the Angel of Death staring you straight in the face. This is one situation where a little knowledge is not a dangerous thing, but quite the opposite. All it takes to become a 'Pinch-hitter' is a couple of hours training with a good instructor, and if that can turn your petrified partner into a keen co-pilot it could turn out to be the best flying investment you ever made. The Aircraft Owners' and Pilots' Association (AOPA) has a suggested syllabus for a Pinch-hitter course and many flying schools and instructors will be happy to take your partner through the short ground school and the couple of hours instruction in the air. That is all that should be necessary to banish this source of worry from your partner's mind and from there on all you have to do is make sure he or she occasionally gets in a bit of practice as a Pinch-hitter. (The term Pinch-hitter, incidentally, derives from the American baseball game, where a Pinch-hitter is someone who comes on to play as a substitute.)

Collision Hazards

One item that never seems to enter the apprehensive passenger's head is the idea that you might bump into another aircraft. We certainly don't want to add yet another worry to those they already have but, as mentioned above, asking passengers to help you keep a good look out makes them feel a useful part of the team and gives them something positive to do during the flight. You should, of course, assure them that the sky is a very big place compared with the restricted space on a roadway and that midair collisions are very rare occurrences indeed.

Had aircraft been developed and used long before cars, what reaction do you imagine an inventor would have received from the general public when he first proposed a new means of transport called an automobile? He would have had to describe it as being rather like a light aircraft with its wings and tail removed. It would travel along narrow bands of asphalt or concrete and would be able to overtake slower automobiles only by steering to miss them by a gap of just a few inches. Oncoming automobiles (with a closing speed of up to around 140mph) would constantly be missing each other by about the same narrow margin. Directional control to enable the 'pilots' of automobiles to aim for these narrow gaps was to be entirely dependent on the grip being maintained between a few square centimetres of rubber and the asphalt surface.

Seasoned pilots and passengers of light aircraft would probably have laughed him out of court; nobody would be so crazy as to risk their lives in a dangerous and impracticable traffic system like that. As the bumper stickers say, I'd rather be flying, it's safer.

Chapter 2

New Horizons

Bigger . . . and in Some Ways Better

The first few ventures you fly as a newly qualified pilot, (taking friends for a trip or visiting a new airfield or three) may well be flown in the same type of aircraft as the one you trained in, quite possibly the self-same aeroplane. It will not be long though before you decide it is time to make the change from flying what is essentially a training tool, to piloting something a bit more like a going places aeroplane. You may be bold enough and wealthy enough to head straight up the scale to a higher power, retractable undercarriage aircraft, possibly with a constant speed propeller. More likely though, you will trade the training Tomahawk for a touring Archer, or swap your Cessna 152 for one of those ubiquitous Cessna 172s or Skyhawks. (New pilots tend to be rather conservative and to stick to types from the manufacturer they know best.)

If you are in the bolder category and are heading straight for a more complex aeroplane, then if you wish you can skip the rest of this section. When you get to Chapter 6 you will find there is a whole section designed to help you adjust to retractable undercarriage aircraft and all the other goodies that usually go with them. For those pilots who would rather make their advance through aeroplane types in more gradual steps, let's look first at what is involved in the move from a trainer to one of the simpler types of touring aircraft. This generally means the change from a two seat to a four seat machine and automatically brings with it rather greater importance to the question of weight and balance of the aeroplane. Aircraft like the Cessna 172, Grumman Traveler, Piper Archer, Aérospatiale Tampico and many others, are advertised and sold as four-seaters but can in fact be used to carry four people within their certified limits of weight and C of G position only if great care is taken. Usually four up is possible only if no baggage is on board or, alternatively, if the fuel tanks are only partially filled. You should therefore never plan on flying this class of aeroplane with four on board to anything approaching its maximum range, without first very carefully checking the all-important weight and balance schedules.

These schedules you will find in the aircraft pilot's operating handbook (POH) and having a good read of this publication is really the best way of starting your conversion from trainer to tourer. Once you have digested the POH you will probably have a few questions to put to a helpful instructor, or to someone who is familiar with piloting the type involved. With the answers to your questions committed to memory, head next for a few minutes quiet contemplation sitting in the new cockpit whilst the aeroplane is sitting on the ground. Get yourself familiar with the new positions of things like the trim wheels, fuel cocks, flap levers, seat adjustments, instrument layout and so on. Then look carefully over what is probably a much more comprehensive avionics installation than you had on the trainer. The radios may well work completely differently; there may be a selector panel that is new to you, and a transponder, GPS, VOR or DME perhaps. Have you ever seen that instrument called an EGT gauge before? There is no point at all in paying to hire and fly an aeroplane with any piece of gear until you know what it can do for you and you are comfortable that you know exactly how to operate it. Get accustomed to entries and exits (normal and emergency) and door and baggage compartment latching. Work through all the checklists for the new aircraft, asking someone if you are unsure of where anything is or how a particular check should be done.

Bigger isn't always Better

When you actually come to fly the new machine you should be prepared for the touring aircraft's improvement in cruising speed; it is likely to be around 15 knots faster than its smaller brethren. Remember though that not all performance differences will be improvements. When a four-seater is loaded close to maximum permitted weight, you will find that the take-off distance required to clear the nominal 50 foot obstacle is appreciably longer (in the case of the Cessna 172, about 300 feet more than is needed for the 152) and that the sea level rate of climb is poorer. During take-off most pilots graduating from two to four seat aircraft are quite surprised at the amount of extra right rudder they need to keep straight; this is one result of having a higher horsepower engine turning a larger diameter propeller. Most of the control forces will feel a bit heavier too and you will soon find that trimming the aircraft is even more helpful to you than it was in your trainer. Proper trimming reduces pilot fatigue and makes it easier to maintain accurate heights and headings . . . and to make consistently smooth landings. The main reason behind this is the higher wing loading of the bigger aircraft; this also makes these types more stable in turbulence and less prone to floating down the runway as some trainer types tend to do. In turn, this sometimes makes the use of a bit of power in the landing round-out useful. It helps you to avoid having the aircraft unexpectedly drop onto the runway with the attitude not quite the way you intended it.

If you decide to make your 'upgrade' change to an aircraft built by a different manufacturer, such as from Tomahawk to Cessna 172 or from Cessna 152 to Grumman Cheetah, you should be prepared for a few additional culture shocks. Your view from the cockpit may be radically altered, for the worse or better, especially whilst in the circuit. As you make your turns, low wings get out of the way to let you see the runway you are heading for, whilst high wings have a nasty habit of hiding the threshold from sight. Gravity-fed fuel, and the need for electric fuel pumps on differing types, must be got used to. Also, you must adjust to the narrower main wheel spread of many high wing aircraft, which makes them a little less stable on the ground in windy conditions than most low wing designs.

Knowing your aeroplane thoroughly is essential for safe flying in whichever type of aircraft you may choose to pilot. Making a point of really getting to know the intimate details of each new aircraft you fly is an excellent habit for you to get into when your PPL is still fairly fresh. It is a habit that will make your later transition to more complex types easier, safer and more satisfying for you.

Feel Comfortable Away from the Circuit

One of the sadder reasons for some pilots losing their enthusiasm for flying, is simply the fact that they are the ones who never pluck up enough courage to venture very far from their home airfield. Doing endless circuits (or even slightly extended tours of the immediate neighbourhood) does soon begin to pall, not only for you as a pilot but also for any passengers who venture up with you more than once.

During your training for the PPL you probably spent most of your airborne time fairly close to the airfield and the local flying area. By the time you got your licence you had become pretty familiar with most of the local landmarks and were reasonably confident of being able to find your way back to base without any difficulties. Your experience of flying elsewhere at that stage was probably no more than a short spell of navigation practice, plus your dual and solo qualifying cross-country flights. You may be one of those pilots who got back to base after flying around that triangular trip with a feeling of some surprise and immense relief that you ever found your way home again. Yet the real purpose of most civil aeroplanes is to convey people and goods expeditiously and safely from one place to another. It rather defeats the object of the exercise if you spend most of your post-PPL flying taking yourself from one place right back to that same place again. It is also unfortunately one of the surest ways of guaranteeing the onset of boredom with flying and the probable lapse of a perfectly good PPL.

Depending on your attitude of mind, reaching out geographically towards new horizons can seem to be either an exhilarating challenge or an unnecessary risk. But refusal to meet the challenge is also to risk losing the licence you have worked so hard to earn. There is a corny old (anonymous) quotation about risk that seems to apply here.

Risk must be taken, because the greatest hazard in life is to risk nothing. The person who risks nothing, does nothing, has nothing . . . Only the person who risks is free.

Flying to faraway places really can be a great experience and, provided you plan and prepare properly for it, the risk of making a fool of yourself by getting lost is really pretty minuscule. A small aeroplane opens up wonderful opportunities for travel to destinations denied to mere ground bound mortals. It is just as easy to fly to offshore islands as it is to drive to neighbouring towns. Crossing the Irish Sea or the English Channel is no longer a major undertaking involving ferry schedules or 'Le Shuttle'. You find many mainland European countries are now within day trip distance of southern England; Ireland is just an hour or so away from northern England or Wales; the Hebrides and northern Isles have become just a couple of hours flying time away from much of Scotland. But to enjoy all these benefits you must first break the mental umbilical cord that seems to tie some pilots to their home airfield.

Keep it Simple to Start With

Gently does it. Don't make your first post-PPL cross-country into a major expedition by choosing a hard to find little grass airfield somewhere at the other end of the country as your destination. That would be as good a way as any of frightening yourself off ever trying anything else. Getting 'uncertain of your position' (as lost is often euphemistically termed) is not difficult to do in any pilot's early days, but if you start your cross-country flying by being well-prepared for an easy trip and work gently up from there you'll do all right. You should be able (most of the time at least) to avoid that sinking feeling of not being quite sure you really are where you think you ought to be. But we have to accept that it does still happen occasionally, even to the best of pilots.

Before even working out a good route, you should check that you know how to operate all the navigational gizmos you have available on the panel. Some flying instructors have an unfortunate habit of explaining little more than the most rudimentary uses of the VOR, DME and ADF during PPL training. You should certainly learn all you can about them before you set off for faraway places; they can be of immense help. If there is a GPS (see Chapter 7) in the aircraft kit (or you are lucky enough to own or can borrow one) master how its knobs and buttons work before you take off. Properly handled, a GPS makes it very, very difficult for a pilot to get thoroughly lost. However, operated without the basic knowledge of their functions and limitations, GPS receivers and moving maps can be downright misleading. Every hour you spend studying the *User's Manual* on the ground, if possible coupled with a bit of practice with the GPS receiver in 'Demo Mode', will be repaid many times over in the air. If you have access to a PC, there are several very useful programs and simulators available (see Chapter 7) which make it easy, and inexpensive, to learn how to make the most of VORs, DMEs and ADFs for navigation whether you are flying VFR or IFR.

Some PC flight simulator programs incorporate good UK scenery which can be reasonably useful as preparation for cross-country flights. Even the programmers would hesitate to claim that all their scenery is really true to life, but some of the best of the add-on UK and other European scenery for the Microsoft FS4 and FS5 flight simulator programs can be good enough to give a real life VFR pilot a pretty good idea of what to look out for on the approach into a new destination airfield. Cities, motorways and main roads, service stations, coastlines, prominent buildings, lakes, power stations and, of course, aerodromes, all appear tolerably lifelike on the monitor screen. A preliminary PC flight along the planned route can sometimes give a newcomer to navigation in the air a slight sense of *déjà vu* when the real landmarks actually turn up later, just as expected, outside the windscreen of the aircraft. There is more about these PC flight simulators in Chapter 7.

Once you have mastered the techniques of using VORs and NDBs, it is a useful insurance to plan your early trips to airfields which have navaids on or close to them. You may never even tune them in, but it is always comforting to know that they are available should your map-reading and dead-reckoning happen to hit a snag. With so much of the UK close to the coastline (the easiest visual navigational feature in the world) picking a first destination that lies close to a well-defined coastal feature is another suggestion you might consider. As you succeed in finding the first few airfields you aim for, your confidence in your own ability will quickly rise and it will all gradually begin to get easier. Soon you will be quite happily setting out for insignificant little grass airstrips tucked away in the midst of lots of other similar looking grass fields that aren't airfields . . . and one day you'll very probably find you just cannot identify the one you are looking for at all. Perhaps your planning this time was . . . er . . . just a little slipshod?

Preparing for the Unexpected

All through your pilot training you will have been made very much aware of the fact that aero-engines are not infallible and that they do occasionally fail in the air. Your instructor's insistence that you continuously search for fields suitable for forced landings without power, all the exercises you had to do in practice forced landings, and the simulated engine failures sprung on you immediately after take-off, all tend to imprint on your mind the idea that the break down of aero-engines must be an almost everyday occurrence. For some impressionable folk this type of training can have a very inhibiting effect on the flying they are prepared to do after qualifying for their PPLs. In aviation's very early days, engines were notoriously unreliable. Running time between failures was almost better measured in minutes rather than hours, and the fact that a pilot arrived on schedule at the end of an hour long flight was something to be commented upon.

Nowadays aircraft engines are, by and large, pretty reliable beasts. Those few that do fail in the air have very often given their pilots clear advance warnings that problems were imminent, warnings that the pilot either didn't understand or simply chose to ignore. An engine that has always been easy to start doesn't suddenly become recalcitrant without some reason, possibly mechanical. A sudden increase in oil or fuel consumption, any anomalous readings on gauges for pressure, the cylinder head temperature or exhaust gas temperature, are all things that ought to be investigated by engineers before the aircraft is ever taken into the air again. Unusual mag drops, rough running, misfiring, oily cowlings can all frequently be signals that something is wrong with the engine's state of health and that you should be looking for expert opinion on the ground rather than risking engine failure in the air.

Statistically, according to AOPA USA, around 200,000 hours are flown for every forced landing that takes place. (These figures relate to forced landings without power, not the ones that are caused by pilots flying into bad weather or getting hopelessly lost and putting down

28

under power into a field.) There seems to be no reason why the ratio should be all that different in European countries. So, statistically, a PPL qualified pilot flying even a generous total of 200 hours per year, could anticipate having to cope with a forced landing roughly once in every thousand years. But, as Mark Twain put it, 'There are three kinds of lies; lies, damned lies and statistics'. Concerning forced landings, I am well aware that this quote is true from personal experience, having had to cope with two forced landings during my first 2,000 hours of piloting. One was due to the fracture of a con-rod in an ancient, but normally very reliable, seven-cylinder Cheetah radial engine. This is one of the few types of engine breakdown that gives the unfortunate pilot no advance warning whatsoever. My second forced landing (virtually without power) was the consequence of the head of a snapped exhaust valve being mangled up inside the cylinder of a Lycoming. I have to admit that particular engine had done its best to let me know that all was not well. It had become tricky to start and wasn't running quite as smoothly as it used to, but foolishly I hadn't interpreted the message it was trying to convey to me. One lives and one learns. The lesson to learn here is that if there is ever any doubt in your mind about the serviceability of an aircraft or its engine, forget any other pressures there may be for you to fly; just don't take the machine into the air. That way, with any luck, you should make a close approach to the statistical 200,000 hours before you have to cope with your first forced landing.

Even if you do happen to draw the short straw and find yourself up in the air one day with a dead engine and a windmilling prop, remember that it isn't by any means the end of the world. If you are flying a fixed undercarriage single-engine aircraft you can console yourself with the thought that 95% of all forced landings in these are brought off successfully without any serious injuries or fatalities to the occupants. In single-engine retractables, for some reason about 10% of the forced landings do result in serious injuries or deaths, and this figure rises to 25% in the case of twins. Even four engine jet airliners occasionally get involved in forced landings and on one memorable occasion in July 1984 a Boeing 767 ran out of fuel yet was safely landed (without injury to any of the 61 on board) on a disused airfield in Manitoba by its Captain Robert Pearson. As luck would have it, he just happened to be an experienced sailplane pilot.

Commonsense Failure Avoidance
The problem experienced by that Air Canada Boeing (running out of fuel) is in fact one of the most common causes of GA aircraft forced landings. It is also one of the most easily avoided. Even more

frustrating are the forced landings that occur due to fuel starvation through the pilot's mismanagement of the fuel system while there is still a perfectly adequate supply of fuel on board. Add to these two causes the engine 'failures' due to pilots who don't apply carburetter heat as soon as necessary when they encounter carburetter icing and you have accounted for over half of all GA forced landings. So if you know how to manage your fuel system, if you make a point of always carrying sufficient fuel for the trip, plus adequate reserves, and if you are able to recognise the symptoms of carb icing and be ready to apply full carb heat whenever these occur, you have already cut your chances of being involved in a forced landing by more than half. About another 10% of all forced landings are caused by fuel contamination, so once again it is in your own hands as the pilot to improve your chances of never being confronted by a forced landing. Make a point of always checking all the fuel tank and sump drains. Make sure there is no water or dirt in the fuel, that it is the correct colour for the grade of avgas (or mogas) that you use and that it has no paraffin smell indicative of avtur contamination. A piston engine will stop immediately pure jet fuel is fed into it, and even a mixture of jet fuel and avgas can cause internal detonation in the cylinders, with consequential risk of major mechanical damage to the engine. It is vital therefore to ensure that piston engine aircraft are never fed the wrong fuel diet. At one time, many turbocharged piston engine aircraft were prominently marked with the word 'Turbo' somewhere on their flanks and this did tend to mislead some refuellers into filling the tanks with fuel appropriate for gas turbine engines. If any aircraft you fly still carries the 'T' word, be especially careful when refuelling... or safer still, remove the offending decal or badge altogether.

If the Worst Comes to the Worst

There remains a statistically tiny possibility that, despite your having done all the correct things to avoid stupid engine failures, you still may be unfortunate enough to encounter an engine with a crankshaft, bearing, con-rod, piston or other normally reliable component that lets you down without warning. Is there any way to prepare for such an eventuality, so that you can maximise your chances of getting away with a forced landing with nothing worse to show for the experience than a muddy pair of shoes from walking through a farmer's field? The first thing, assuming it isn't an engine failure at low altitude, is to trim the aircraft to its best gliding speed then run through the 'engine failure in flight' checklist. This is one checklist you really ought to commit to memory and rehearse from time to time; the moment just after everything goes quiet is not the time to have to start thumbing through an owner's manual looking for it. If the engine has stopped in a cloud of oil or with a sudden mechanical clunk, if the prop has parted company with the crankshaft, or some other obviously terminal failure has occurred (or if you know you really are stupid enough to have run out of fuel) get on to the next stage directly and start looking for a landing place. Otherwise check the mag switches, change tanks, try each mag separately, change mixture settings, switch to hot air, use the fuel booster pump if there is one, and follow the rest of that check list. You never know, it might be possible to bring the dead engine back to life. Once you have completed all this, if time permits and you still have enough altitude to stand a chance of being heard, put out a distress call to enable ATC to alert rescue services for you.

If the engine refuses to restart, where is the best place for you to land? All your practice forced landings were probably aimed at the most suitable looking piece of farmland in the vicinity because that has much better training value than the best place for a forced landing. This is usually an aerodrome if there happens to be one in the vicinity. (This does not apply if the emergency you are involved with is an engine failure immediately after take-off. You almost certainly won't make it back to the field you've just left, so don't even try. The only helpful policy to counteract this situation is always to make it a habit to gain as much height as you can as quickly as possible after take-off.) If you are high enough and have a GPS receiver with the 'nearest facility' feature, you might want to use it to find out how far, and in which direction, is the nearest airfield. The fairly typical four-seat, 150 hp single engine aircraft I usually fly can, at its best glide speed, cover more than seven miles from 4,000 feet with the prop windmilling. (Like most light aircraft it will glide farther if you can stop the prop windmilling, when it produces less drag.) It is thus quite often possible to reach and land at an aerodrome lying several miles away from where the engine quits.

Failing that, a disused aerodrome can be a good bet, although you will have to be careful about the hazards which may exist at some of these. The fact that the tarmac or concrete surface of the runways will probably have deteriorated badly, is not of too much importance when you are making an emergency landing, but what looks like an attractive place to put down can have hidden traps for the unwary. Farmers have often erected fences across the old runways to control livestock, and they also have an awkward tendency to store all manner of things on or alongside them, things that may not initially be all that obvious from the air. The approaches to disused runways are, of course, no longer inspected to ensure they are free from obstructions, so beware of wires, masts etc that may make a normal approach tricky. If you happen to be involved in making a precautionary landing at a disused airfield, as opposed to a forced landing with a dead engine, you should always try to take the opportunity of having a close look at the approach and the condition of the runway by making a low fly-past before you commit yourself to actually landing there. Disused runways are usually marked with a white diagonal St Andrew's cross at each end, but with the passage of time, these can become difficult to spot from aloft. Certain former military aerodromes also have a white bar underlining the cross. This indicates that the runway has been inspected within the last six months and was, at that time, considered to be suitable to land on in an emergency. It isn't a guarantee, however, that the whole runway is safe for you to use on the particular day you happen to need it!

Failing an Airfield, try a Farmer's Field
The next best place for an emergency landing is any decent sized flattish field, preferably with any trees or other obstructions at the upwind end (ie the far end, when you are landing into wind) where your aircraft will be travelling slowly. I've often heard it argued that a motorway or main road would be better than a field, smoother, pretty level and with outside assistance readily on hand. True, up to a point, but hitting a truck head-on is not a recipe for success, nor is tangling with lighting standards or those well-nigh invisible wires and cables that festoon many roadsides. A nasty aircraft/vehicle coming-together could also keep lawyers working happily for months, at your expense.

You should aim to reach the vicinity of your chosen field with the aircraft clean and with some height to spare. You ought to avoid any rapid or harsh control inputs while trying to reach your chosen landing place, remembering that in hectic manoeuvring the drag effect of hefty aileron, elevator and rudder deflections can lose you as much height as lowering the flaps does. Manoeuvre to arrive at a marker-point representative of the end of a normal downwind leg at 1,000 feet agl, using flaps, lowering undercarriage or sideslipping as necessary to shed any excess height. The goal you are aiming for is to arrive over the threshold, in a controlled condition, but not flying any faster than the normal short field threshold speed before you contact the surface. The pre-landing checks should include closing the main fuel cock, turning off the ignition and pulling back the mixture to idle cut-off position. The master-switch should be left on until all electrical requirements (radio, flaps, undercarriage etc) have been dealt with. Whether or not to lower the wheels of a retractable is very much a matter of judgement, depending on the type of surface; if it is rough, a wheels-up landing is generally the safer choice for those on board, though not necessarily for the machinery.

Landing as close into wind as possible and using the approach and threshold speeds you have been taught for short field landings is not a bad formula. It minimises your speed relative to the ground and thus the deceleration forces involved. Another rule worth following, that will certainly help your chances of walking off unscathed after a forced landing, is to borrow from car practice and always wear a shoulder harness when flying. If the forced landing does result in a sharp deceleration, anyone wearing just a lap-strap is going to end up like the dummies you see in the slow-motion car accident films. Your body bends in the middle as your torso jerks forward, then, as the lap-strap cuts into your spare tyre, your head starts heading for your feet, but is thwarted en route by the instrument panel, which imprints itself onto your face. Luckily, the majority of forced landings do not involve deceleration forces as violent as car crashes, and this actually makes them more survivable for the occupants. Unless you are unlucky enough to fly into something like rocks, a cliff, a big tree or a substantial wall on final approach, your touch down from controlled flight at normal sink rate and threshold speed should result, even on a rough or sloping surface, in a much gentler stop than the average car to car head-on collision. The aeroplane may well shed bits and pieces as it decelerates, but crushing airframe components help to cushion occupants and in a single engine aircraft, that solid lump of engine ahead of the cockpit forms a useful battering ram that helps to protect those on board. Remember that the primary objective in a forced landing is to ensure the survival of the occupants. The aeroplane itself is of comparatively minor importance. If all the occupants survive, it is a successful forced landing; if they all survive uninjured, it is an excellent forced landing; if the aircraft also ends up undamaged, it is a perfect forced landing.

After-landing Actions
Once you are safely down, even though fire is a remote possibility unless fuel tanks are ruptured, it is as well to exit the aircraft quickly. Don't desert it altogether though. Have someone look after it if possible, whilst someone else goes to search for help, the police or a telephone. The aircraft insurance policy may well include a clause saying the aircraft must be safeguarded as far as possible following any forced landing. Some insurers will reimburse reasonable costs incurred in doing this too, so perhaps you could afford to call Group 4 or Securicor after you've informed the police and ATC of your predicament! That settled, you have only to wipe the mud off your shoes and try to hitch a lift back to the airfield.

Keeping Things in Proportion

Expecting the unexpected is a good maxim in flying; it helps you stay one step ahead of the game, which is a much safer place to be than always trying to catch up with a situation. At the same time, though, you must keep things in perspective. Even though a great deal of your instructional time will have been spent on teaching you how to cope with engine failures, most pilots go through their entire flying lives without ever having to put that training into practice. Fear of losing an engine in the air should never be allowed to restrict the amount or the type of flying you do once you have your PPL. Being well prepared to cope with this eventuality if it ever were to happen to you is an excellent thing. Planning all your flying in constant apprehension of such a remote contingency is a different matter entirely. Your chances of a major prize in the National Lottery are probably statistically greater than the chances of you ever encountering that sudden ominous silence in the air.

Planning Ahead

Dozens of text books are available which deal in detail with the subject of flight planning. This chapter has not been written to take their place. The idea here is to make a few suggestions about some things you might be forgiven for overlooking in your first few ventures away from home base. Once you have decided where you are going, whether it is a 20 minute trip for a cup of coffee or a month long holiday journey traversing half a continent, make sure your flight bag contains all the maps, charts, frequency information and flight guides needed to cover the route. And in particular, make sure they are all up to date current editions. Don't get hemmed in by carrying inadequate map cover. The whole route from Retford to Caernarfon, for instance, is on the CAA 1:500,000 chart for Northern England and Northern Ireland. But what if some unforecast nasty low stuff drifts in on you from the north-west whilst you are in the air? Wouldn't it be nice to have the Southern England chart with you too, just in case you feel the need to divert to some cloud free aerodrome lying awkwardly for you a few miles off the bottom of your Northern chart?

However good the weather may be, always have at least one alternate destination in mind before you set out. And have its landing information, frequencies etc all to hand too. Mark your route clearly on the chart and if you are embarking on a longish trip, sometimes it is worth marking a second 'bad-weather' route too, in case perhaps thunderstorms develop or the cloud decides to cover the hills along the route you originally intended to fly. Don't allow controlled airspace to scare you away from the route you would really prefer to fly. Air Traffic Controllers are actually quite human and only if they are really busy will they refuse you entry to any controlled airspace that is open to VFR traffic. It usually helps if your aircraft is transponder equipped. That is another piece of equipment (again often skimmed over lightly by PPL instructors) which you really ought to spend some time getting familiar with before you set off on any serious cross-country stuff. Naturally, if you always timidly plan your routes so they go around any CTR, MATZ or TMA and so never have to talk to ATC or ask for clearance through their bit of airspace, you'll never find out how co-operative they can be. Nobody will be very co-operative however if you disregard the regulations concerning any Airways, Prohibited, Restricted and Danger Areas, parachuting and gliding sites, active ATZs and instrument approach lanes etc. Check your chart for these and other kindred restrictions and obstructions. It is always worth bearing in mind the existence of Danger Area crossing and advisory services. You don't have to look any farther than the bottom of your half-million charts to find out about the DACS and DAAIS. Make use of them.

Cross-countrys Should be Fun

Remember too that you are now flying for pleasure; there is nothing in any section of the Air Navigation Order or the Rules of the Air that says you must always fly the direct route from A to B. If there is a historic castle or a motor-racing circuit, nudist colony, chalk hill figure, cathedral or even perhaps a spectacular bit of cliff scenery that might interest you or your passengers, why not go and see it? Take your camera along, enjoy your flight. The world is full of sights and spectacles denied to ordinary groundlings but which look superb when seen from aloft. Don't become so fascinated with the scenery below that you forget to keep a good look out for other aircraft though. You may not be the only pilot having a look-see at the Humber Bridge or the Old Man of Hoy that afternoon. And so far as that racing circuit is concerned, if it is active remember your minimum height rules for flying in the vicinity of crowds.

Flight Plans

There is of course, the other type of Flight Plan, that official piece of paper CA48/RAF F2919 (and its equivalents as issued by foreign aviation authorities). For some obscure reason there are quite a few PPL pilots I know who have a horror of these FPLs. I am sure it is sometimes more the worry about having to complete one of these forms correctly that dissuades them from going abroad, rather than any worries they may have about flying across a stretch of salt water. In practice, as soon as you have done the job a couple of times, filing a VFR flight plan becomes simplicity itself. In some countries, such as Belgium, Denmark and Switzerland, so many private VFR flights cross international borders that almost every private pilot is accustomed to completing Flight Plans regularly for most of his or her flights. In this country, so far as VFR flights in aircraft with a maximum take-off weight which does not exceed 5,700 kg it is mandatory to complete a Flight Plan only for flights to or from the UK which will cross the UK FIR boundary. (Flights within the Scottish and London Upper FIR also require FPLs but since the Upper FIR has its base at Flight Level 245, this is highly unlikely to concern many readers of this book.) Any VFR flight within Class D airspace control zones or control areas also requires a flight plan but it is perfectly acceptable to comply with this requirement simply by passing details of the flight to the appropriate ATC unit by radio while you are in the air.

To File or nor to File?

There are other occasions when it is advisable to file a FPL even though there is no compulsion to do so. Common sense should tell you when. Sensible hill walkers and mountaineers leave details of their planned route with some responsible person before they head for the mountains, so that if they don't get back to civilization as planned, somebody has at least a rough idea of where to start searching for them. Similarly, sensible flyers don't set out to cross inhospitable terrain (mountains, water, wilderness or desert) without filing a flight plan, for precisely the same reasons. Finally, there is nothing to prevent a pilot from filing a Flight Plan at his or her own discretion for any flight.

Completing the form is not difficult and there are many leaflets, posters and books to help any pilot who is new to the job to learn the basic steps involved. If in doubt, get hold of the CAA's General Aviation Safety Sense Leaflet 20 which clearly shows you how.

Flying Vacations

Possibly not the first summer after you get your PPL, but sometime not too long after that, you are quite likely to begin mulling over the notion of combining your annual holiday with some flying. There are certainly a few complications involved, but none of these is insurmountable and you shouldn't let them put you off what can turn out to be an excellent way of making good use of your licence. Most clubs, and many groups, ask for a certain minimum number of flying hours per day to justify doing without their machine for a period, but provided the figure asked for is not unreasonable, it should equate with what you intend doing anyway. If it doesn't, you probably haven't planned your holiday properly to ensure that it really justifies your use of the aeroplane in the first place.

There are many marvellous flying holiday destinations within the UK, but many pilots plan their first flying vacation for places that are generally reputed (but alas, don't always turn out to be) warmer and sunnier than Britain. France is undoubtedly the favourite destination for British pilots but Spain has many aficionados too, as have Belgium, the Netherlands, Germany and, in recent years, some of the eastern European countries. Before you set out for any such destination, you must get acquainted with all the differences that exist between the UK flying regulations that you know and love, and the VFR rules of the country you are heading for . . . and of all the others whose airspace you are likely to be passing through. Europe is much more unified than it used to be but despite JAA and all the other international bodies, each State's aviation authority is still tending to hang on to a different set of VFR rules. This may well change within the next few years but meantime these variations still affect such things as: the UK's Quadrantal Rule (unknown elsewhere in Europe where the semi-circular rule largely takes its place); circuit joining procedures; night flying; SVFR limits and VFR in airways (not by any means always forbidden as it is in UK airspace). More detailed information on some of these matters is contained in Chapter 4 of this book under 'Other Countries; Other Customs'. Even the language used by ATC in some places can be foreign to you. Despite English being the language of international aviation, many French and German aerodromes (especially the smaller ones) often use their native tongues for VHF transmissions. Fortunately, however, at many of these airfields the controller can also muster up enough English to cope with pilots unable to speak his or her language.

Don't let yourself be deterred from going because of these differences. There would be little point in bothering to fly abroad at all if everything there were to be precisely the same as it is at home. Just be prepared and learn as much as possible about the variations to expect before you get there. *Pooley's* has some useful information in their *European Guides* and all the up to date facts are to be found in the AIPs for the countries concerned. If all of this seems to be rather too much to master straight away, you could make a simpler start by trying an 'overseas' flying holiday across the water to the Isle of Man,

Guernsey, Mull or Orkney perhaps. Save up all those other lovely island airfields like Belle Isle, Texel, Sylt or Corsica for later, once you have had time to get all the facts together. One useful way of preparing for a trip like this is to read about other pilots' experiences on similar ventures. *Pilot* magazine for example publishes many reports on foreign destinations and copies of many of the relevant back numbers are usually available.

Fly While There Without Flying There

A slight variation on the self-piloted flying holiday theme is well worth considering. This consists of travelling first by airline or surface transport and then renting an aircraft at your destination. Usually, outside of Europe, it is necessary to obtain a local validation of your UK PPL. Except in a few countries this presents no great problem, other than perhaps swotting up enough about local air law to pass a written or oral test. In the case of the United States, an FAA Airman's License can be obtained on the strength of your CAA PPL before you leave the UK, but before you can legally use this on an American registered aircraft you first must pass the FAA's Biennial Flight Review. With the appropriate formalities for the country concerned behind you, all that remains for you to do is to convince a QFI at a club or school that you can actually fly the machine you want to rent. Then for a few dollars more (or lire, francs or what-have-you) you have a whole new sky to explore. I have enjoyed renting aircraft for vacations like this in many countries including Italy, France, Sweden, the United States, Canada and New Zealand. For the relatively little amount of advance preparation involved, this type of flying can bring an immense amount of pleasure and it often enormously extends the horizons of a holiday in foreign parts, not just for the pilot but for the whole family.

Navigation Know-how

Psychologists claim that few people are ever afraid of anything they thoroughly understand. It is awareness of the unknown that causes a great deal of anxiety. If you are just the tiniest bit afraid of getting lost should you venture into the air outside the local area, this is possibly caused by an instinctive feeling that you don't yet know enough about navigation. Navigation is a vast subject and one about which most sensible pilots continue to increase their knowledge all through their flying lives. One paramount rule for an inexperienced pilot is always to plan carefully ahead. Another is to be ready to admit it if, despite all your planning, things don't work out as you had expected. Should you begin to get that uneasy feeling that you may not actually be quite where you think you ought to be, follow a sensible routine. Firstly, note down the present time, the last positive pinpoint you identified and work out how far you should be from there. Check that the Directonal Indicator (DI) still agrees with the compass. When searching the chart for where you might be, remember always to work from the ground to the chart. Identify something outside the aircraft, then try to find it on the map; don't pick some feature on the map and try to spot it on the ground. That seldom works. And while you are looking for some distinctive coast, railway, motorway, river or the like, you should try to maintain both your route plan heading and your good look out for other aircraft.

If you do get lost, tell someone. Don't wait until the fuel runs low or darkness becomes imminent; that simply compounds the difficulties for everyone concerned. Transmit to whichever ground station you have been working and tell them quite clearly that you are lost. There is no point in talking round the situation and this is no time for false pride. If you can get no reply from that station, go straight onto the Emergency frequency 121.50MHz and make a PAN call. If you have a transponder on board, switch it to squawk Code 7700. That will help the Emergency Service to pick you up on radar and give you all possible assistance to get safely down again, either at your destination or elsewhere.

Preventing yourself from getting lost is of course much better than any cure such as this. As already mentioned, one of the best safeguards is always to be equipped with the correct charts for the job. It doesn't matter if you have the very latest in electronic moving map GPS gizmos on board; these can break down, batteries can run flat and their programs can be corrupted much more easily than a good old-fashioned paper chart. Old-fashioned, perhaps, but not old; charts go out of date (just as moving map databases do) and the only one worth having on board is the latest, current issue. A couple of new UK half-million charts to cover a route you plan to fly will cost you the equivalent of about 20 minutes flying time in a typical four-seat single. They could well save you considerably more than 20 minutes of aimlessly wandering around in the air looking for where you are without the appropriate chart. It is also against the law, incidentally, to fly without having all the charts you need for your flight and for any diversion you might have to make.

Which chart?
Most purposes are best served by the standard ICAO 1:500,000 scale charts issued by the CAA, but for more detailed information about

what you are flying over, there is also a useful 1:250,000 scale series available. It is not, however, obligatory to use the CAA published charts. Jeppesen have an excellent series designed for the VFR pilot who uses GPS, but equally useful to the pilot who has no access to satellite navigation. These charts have the advantage that all the cartographical detail, map symbols and the whole presentation are the same for all countries in Europe. It can sometimes get a bit confusing if you have to switch from the UK version of the ICAO chart, with which you have become familiar, to a French or perhaps a German equivalent. You are liable to find that spot heights and contours may sometimes be given in metres instead of feet; the symbol for a glider airfield is totally different; the colours used to indicate controlled airspace, airways and danger areas are perhaps based on a convention that is strange to you. Early pilots did all their flying with the aid of maps out of atlases and motoring maps, there being nothing else available. With no information to add to these, other than the location of aerodromes, in those far off days this was reasonably satisfactory. Nowadays however (although I do know some French and Belgian pilots who still do most of their navigation with the aid of nothing more than marked up Michelin road maps) up-to-date charts produced specifically for aviation really are essentials for safe flying.

The equivalent of about another 20 minutes flying time will get you a good book you should take along with you too, one or other of the VFR flight guides that are now available. 'Never fly without your Pooleys' has been a good advertising maxim for many years now, but if you prefer the layout of a *Bottlang* manual, AFE's *UK VFR Flight Guide* or one of the IFR guides such as *Aerad* or *Jeppesen* to that of *Pooley's Flight Guide*, the choice is yours. In general my advice would be to pick a VFR guide which has an amendment service that allows you to keep it up to date throughout its year of validity. Like charts (and GPS moving map databases) an out-of-date flight guide can cause a lot of confusion when frequencies have changed, runways been closed, navaids moved, or any of the many other changes which constantly plague aviation and which may have taken place since your source was last updated.

Getting all this equipment ready for the flight involves you in quite a few preparatory steps. If the guide book is of the loose-leaf variety it is often useful to extract those pages likely to be relevant and to keep them ready for use, perhaps in a transparent plastic pocket loose-leaf book. After the flight, don't forget to put these pages back in order so you can find them again easily next time you need them for another expedition. Concerning the charts, exterminate all evidence of your earlier flights by erasing the lines relating to them. If you don't, it is all too easy when busy in the cockpit for your eye to pick out the wrong line (one left over from an earlier flight) and this is almost guaranteed to cause a fine old muddle in your mind as you try to sort things out again. Even such a small thing as folding the charts in a suitable manner before take-off, so that the whole length of your track line is going to be easy to get at, is well worthwhile. Wrestling in a small cockpit with sheets of paper up to four feet square is something a pilot can well do without.

Now You See it ...
Only experience will tell you which of the features on a chart make good way points and landmarks and which don't. The difference between good and bad features also varies, depending very much on where you happen to be flying. A motorway may well be a prominent feature in some parts of Scotland, but throughout industrial areas of Germany for example, there are simply so many *Autobahns* that the poor pilot is hard pressed to tell one from another. Big lakes or forests can be good landmarks in many parts of England but over large tracts of Sweden say, it is extremely tricky to tell these apart. Middle-sized towns are, in general, reasonable pinpoints, often positively identifiable from the angles at which roads and railways enter and leave them, but large cities and conurbations are pretty useless. With these you also have to remember legal limits about the minimum heights you are allowed to overfly them. Often conspicuous from the air are aerodromes, disused as well as active. But beware; in some parts of the world (eastern England in particular) there are so many disused airfields dating from WW2 that they can easily be confused, unless some other distinctive feature close to them ensures positive identification. Grass airfields too often look much more prominent on the chart than they do in the countryside below. Finally, please be careful about using any active aerodrome as a pinpoint, since they are all liable to be busy with other aircraft flying in their vicinity. Sometimes aerodromes have specified Visual Reporting Points (VRPs) to help ATC route VFR aircraft into or across controlled airspace and to keep them away from otherwise unprotected instrument approaches. Normal practice is for ATC to ask you to 'report VRP such-and-such' but it is not necessary actually to overfly the VRP. They will generally be quite happy to hear you report '2nm east abeam so-and-so VRP' and this can help avoid congestion over the VRPs. On the other hand, if asked to enter or leave a CTR via a specified entry/exit point you are expected to identify that point on your chart and to overfly it.

Avoid Elementary Errors

Having finished your preflight planning, ensured all the charts and documents are accessible in the cockpit (and legible), included in your preflight inspection removal of dust, flies and streaks from the windshield (to give yourself a fighting chance of actually seeing some of the landmarks you have chosen to use) you are finally ready to get airborne. It is amazing how often low-hours pilots (and even one or two pilots who certainly don't come into this category) come unstuck in their navigation at this early stage. A DI that hasn't been correctly aligned with the magnetic compass can oh so easily lead an unwary pilot off in an entirely wrong direction. So can dyslexic-type confusion between steering 03 and 30 on the DI. Tracks of 130 and 310 have also been known to get crossed in pilots' minds and map-reading VFR pilots have been known to set off, happily following a nice prominent line feature like the M1 motorway or the river Rhine for quite long distances, before it dawns on them that they have been following it in the wrong direction! Do an early check of compass, direction of the sun (assuming you can see it) and an unmistakable landmark, to make sure that sort of thing doesn't happen to you. And concerning the DI, never forget that it precesses (wanders off) in the course of a flight and should always be checked as part of the regular 10 to 15 minute FREDA checks, (Fuel; Radio; Engine Instruments; DI; Altimeter).

RT Unease

During your training for the PPL you will have learned sufficient about the basics of RT useage to pass the radiotelephony exam and your instructor will have introduced you to the standard radio procedures you needed to use for flying in your home airfield environment. If you did your training at a major airport, complete with Tower, Approach, Radar etc frequencies to cope with, and with controlled airspace around it, then you probably gained sufficient familiarity with your VHF radio to enable you to do most of your future VFR flying radio work with ease. You certainly had a heavier cockpit workload during training, than a pilot who was brought up to PPL standard at a quiet little airfield with no more than perhaps a Flight Information Service (Information) or an Aerodrome Air/Ground Communications Service (Radio), but you will reap the benefits of this experience as soon as you start venturing farther from home in your PPL flying. If, on the other hand, you are one of those pilots who, as a student, seldom did more on the radio than talk to the local airfield information service you may well soon find yourself within the ranks of the PPL pilots who would do almost anything rather than get involved with having to talk to strange Air Traffic Controllers. And that inhibition can seriously cramp your style as a pilot, especially in a country like the UK where so much of the airspace is chock-a-block with CTRs, TMAs, MATZs, radar services and the like.

For instance, I know of pilots who, faced with a south/north trip up England, refuse to go anywhere near the east coast for the simple reason that they have heard it is covered with terrible things called LARS (Lower Airspace Radar Services). Since this would mean their having to communicate with fast-talking military controllers they head instead for a complex route through the Midlands or west coast, carefully steering around the Birmingham and East Midlands airspace, or creeping along the Manchester Low-level Corridor and avoiding like the plague any airspace where someone might want to talk to them. They have missed the whole point about ATC and RT. Radiotelephony is designed to allow pilots and ground personnel to communicate with each other, and its primary purpose is to assist the safe and expeditious operation of aircraft. Whilst it is perfectly legal (and often very pleasant) to fly in much of the airspace over most countries without even switching your VHF radio on, it is pretty dumb not to make full use of RT when it can make your flight so much safer and appreciably easier.

Shyness about transmitting on VHF is perhaps understandable in the very early days of training, but a good instructor should ensure that confidence has replaced this reticence long before the student is let loose as a private pilot. If not, however, all is not lost. There are ways of making you talk, however self-conscious you may feel about it.

Don't be Shy
Learning the correct phraseology to use is important for two reasons. The first is for flight safety, to ensure that you transmit in such a way that confusion or misunderstandings do not occur. The second is simply to help make you feel you are not a little outsider in the great big world of aviation airwaves. The basic phraseology is laid down clearly in the CAA's Radiotelephony Manual (CAP 413) but if you find that difficult to digest it is always possible to assimilate RT technique through your ears. Not just while you are in the air, but also at home or elsewhere, it is easy to immerse yourself from time to time in the babble of air traffic communications simply by tuning in an appropriate frequency on a VHF band receiver. If you can afford a VHF transceiver (see Chapter 7) so much the better, but simple airband receivers and scanners suitable for this type of listening-in are available at prices from as little as £20 upwards. By listening to the professionals'

patter you soon get a better 'feel' for what is expected from you as a pilot and you become less likely to make yourself feel awkward or annoy others on the frequency. Neither will you then be so liable to take up valuable air time unnecessarily the way one notorious pilot did who used to sign off his transmissions with something like 'Piper Warrior Golf Bravo Bravo Lima Tango message received, roger, wilco, over and out, good evening.' Eavesdropping like this also helps you anticipate what ATC is likely to say next and what response you will be expected to come up with. You should also hear from time to time the well-worn phrase 'say again', which is one for you to bear very much in mind. Any time you are left in any way uncertain of what message ATC has directed to you, don't guess, don't ignore it, don't assume anything, just transmit 'Say again' until you are sure of the meaning of the message.

On the other hand, you will also hear a lot on the RT that does not conform to CAP 413 standards. There are times when informality creeps into RT, times when you can get away with little chats, but until you get the 'feel' for it, you are better to avoid the informality you will hear from some professional pilots as you listen in on the airband. Once you get into RT practice you will begin to recognise the circumstances when it may be permissable to diverge slightly from the standard phraseology. Don't try to copy the laid-back style of some airline captains, don't intersperse your call with lots of ums and ahs and ers. Think what you are going to say before you press the transmit button and then say it distinctly and not too quickly. That way everyone listening will probably know you are a relatively new PPL pilot, but what the hell; the people who need to know, will understand exactly what they need to know, which is the whole idea of the exercise. You will find that ATC are your friends, and ATC with radar can at times be the pilot's best friend of all.

What advantages does competence in use of the radio bring for you? Many. Psychologically you feel better, not having a small corner of this piloting business that you are uncertain about always niggling away at the back of your mind. Practically, you can now plan cross-country flights without the constraint of trying to avoid having to talk to anyone you don't know. You still won't know who you are talking to, except as a code name like 'Littlefield Radio' or 'Le Touquet Approach', but you will know how to talk to them and how to get them to help you with your flying.

Know What is on Offer

Get to know which types of service ATC can give you. Outside of controlled airspace (or in the 'open FIR' as it is called) you can be flying in Class F or Class G airspace. Here you are entitled to, at the very least, a Flight Information Service (FIS). Under FIS the controller will be able to help you with weather information, details about current serviceability of navaids, activity state of certain Danger Areas and general safety information to help you with your flight. The only traffic information that can be passed to you is about other aircraft in contact with the FIS so this is far from a comprehensive service. Another form of non-radar service is Procedural Service which provides separation between all participating aircraft. The term is not normally used except by military controllers and then only when Procedural Service is for some reason being given as a substitute for Radar Advisory Service. There is one other non-radar service available for your use, but I hope you won't have much call to use it. This is Alerting Service, offered when the controller suspects, or knows because you have told him, that search and rescue assistance is required and he notifies the appropriate people. Then there are the services that a controller with access to radar can offer. These include Radar Information Service (RIS), where the controller warns you of any conflicting traffic but it is up to you to decide what avoiding action, if any, to take. This is an excellent service to use when flying in busy airspace, since the controller acts as a sort of extra look out for you, whilst still letting you get on with your flight without interruptions for what may be unnecessary avoiding action. Under Radar Advisory Service (RAS) on the other hand, the controller will pass you advice on what avoiding action to take. You can elect not to take it (perhaps to avoid getting into cloud) but you must let him know if you don't follow the advice given, since this could put you too close to other traffic you don't know about. Other very useful services available to you whilst flying in the 'Open FIR' include the Lower Airspace Radar Service (LARS) mentioned above, which is really only a service offering pilots either RIS or RAS and, as is the case with other ATC units, it is up to you as pilot to contact them first and ask for whichever type of service it is that you require. Most controllers are very cooperative and friendly men and women, but they aren't psychic, so they can't read your mind to find out what it is you want from them. (Actually, they will generally try to provide the best service available to you at the time if you fail to tell them precisely what you want. Generous people, aren't they?) You can also make use of the MATZ Penetration Service, Danger Area Activity Information Service (DAAIS) and Danger Area Crossing Service (DACS). It is well worth while getting to know all the various forms of help available to you and the CAA has published an excellent Safety Sense leaflet on the subject (No 8) 'Air Traffic Services in the Open FIR'.

Sometimes a student pilot gets to the end of his or her training with the false impression that the folk in the control tower think they are some kind of superior beings. Their main purpose in life sometimes appears to have been to make things difficult for pilots, especially pilots learning to fly light aircraft. They keep you waiting on the ground at holding points while the bill for flying mounts up by the minute; they force you to extend downwind just as you thought you had the circuit working out nicely or, even worse, they make you do some orbits to the left to let instrument traffic land ahead of you. Most of them demand specific information from you before they let you fly through 'their' bit of the sky. But the plain fact is that they are there to provide a service, just as much to you as to other airspace users. Any time you need it, make sure you know how to make full use of it.

Flying a small aeroplane in radio silence through uncluttered skies on a fine clear sunny day can be idyllic, reminiscent of the good old days of flying in the interwar years, but to get the full benefit out of a light aircraft as a means of getting from one place to another pilots these days really have to be competent and relaxed in their use of VHF radiotelegraphy.

Chapter 3

Weather Factors

Know Your Limitations

Many student pilots find meteorology far and away the most complicated subject that they have to study for their PPL examination. On
the other hand many also find it fascinating to learn to understand,
perhaps for the first time in their lives, something about weather
systems, anticyclones, warm fronts and the like. Weather has always
been a feature of our lives of course, an inevitable topic of conversa-
tion and something that affects our work, and possibly our hobbies and
holidays. It certainly is going to affect every PPL pilot's hobby of flying
because it is no exaggeration to say that for any pilot, weather really
can be a matter of life and death.

It is an unfortunate fact that weather is involved as a main or
contributory factor in a very high proportion of all GA accidents.
People continue to die; because the pilot doesn't understand enough
about meteorology to interpret aviation weather data correctly;
because he or she understands it but fails to correlate it sensibly with
his or her flying ability; or simply because the pilot foolishly opts to
press on, deliberately ignoring an adverse forecast of conditions which
are likely to be outside his or her limitations. It is crass stupidity to
pretend to understand a met report, or the print-out of a forecast, if
you have only a vague idea of what '22005KT 2500 BKN005 OVC010'
and so on, actually means. You owe it to yourself, never mind your
unsuspecting passengers, to keep on top of this vital subject. And it is
bordering on criminal if you make a wilful decision to fly into conditions you know are likely to be beyond you. Yet pilots keep on doing
these idiotic things, often getting away with it admittedly, but sometimes sadly adding to the weather-related aviation accident statistics.

Why do pilots do it? The reasons are numerous, but none amounts
to anything approaching a valid excuse for risking your own and your
passengers' necks in the one-sided contest of you against the ruthless
and powerful forces of adverse weather. Sometimes it is a matter of

cash. To abandon the flight would perhaps mean hotel bills, extra hire charges on the aircraft, etc. Sometimes it is business. But would the world (or even your job) really come to an end if you phoned up and said you couldn't get to that meeting? It might well come to an end permanently so far as you were concerned if you gave your presence at a meeting priority over prudence as a pilot. Sometimes it is simply a matter of not losing face. You are a pilot aren't you, not a chicken? Real pilots don't give up when there is a little bit of low cloud or a forecast of thunderstorms or icing about, do they? But, yes, the fact is that real VFR pilots do just that thing. They realise that losing face is infinitely preferable to losing their life, which can quite often be the only realistic option.

Personal Limitations
The limitations for VFR flight in various Classes of airspace are legally laid down and every pilot should know them. But these need not necessarily be your own personal limitations. Only you know whether you are comfortable with the idea of finding a strange airfield in low visibility. The vis may be well within VFR legal limits but still be beyond your personal ones. Are you competent to handle a forecast crosswind at the destination aerodrome which comes close to the demonstrated limit of the aircraft? If not, don't set out for it. Honesty comes into the equation here. Just because other PPL pilots are doing things and seem to be getting away with them doesn't mean that you can, or should, or must, emulate them. The world of flying doesn't generally have policemen on hand to stop you from killing yourself. The one person who has the power to restrain you from doing something foolish is your own self as a prudent pilot. Don't let the pressures of family commitments, business appointments or financial economy override your own sensible judgement as an airman.

Wherever you decide your personal limits lie in terms of visibility, acceptable crosswinds and cloud ceilings, there are two limitations every private pilot who flies any light aircraft should invariably adhere to. Always stay well clear of any bit of the sky where icing conditions are forecast and never ever even begin to think that you and your little aircraft are any match for a thunderstorm. You may be able to cope with the torrential rain (although that can be heavy enough to drown a piston engine and associated hailstones can shatter windshields and damage airframes too) the lightning is unlikely to cause you or the aircraft any serious damage, the thunder is totally innocuous... but the air currents, turbulence, wind shear and down-draughts found within and around a thundercloud, can contain the energy equivalent of a nuclear bomb or two. These forces are quite capable of tearing airliners to pieces, and I am not talking only of tropical thunderstorms either; a Fokker airliner was downed by a thunderstorm over Rotterdam in the 1980s. Light aircraft stand virtually no chance of survival in the maelstrom that is the interior of a cumulonimbus cloud.

Good judgement is deciding to go by car or train or scheduled airliner when the weather doesn't look like being within your limitations. Poor judgement is setting out anyway, just to 'have a look-see', when you know full well that in the end that is bound to commit you to trying to complete the flight. Good judgement is stopping somewhere to top up the tanks when the weather at the destination looks doubtful. Bad judgement is deciding not to bother because a refuelling stop would take too long. Good judgement is waiting until the next TAFs are issued, rather than pressing on with the idea of picking up the latest weather from Volmet en route. Good judgement is part of good airmanship and is probably the best form of life insurance that any pilot can have.

Your personal limitations can vary from day to day. Waken up tired after a long hard day and a short night's sleep and you may feel that you aren't really quite sharp enough to tackle conditions you would normally cope with quite happily. Again, be honest with yourself. And remember that in this matter of making sensible weather-related decisions about limits, two heads are *not* better than one. Put two pilots of roughly equal experience and qualifications in one aeroplane and you will often find that neither wants to be the first one to throw in the towel. As a result both can find themselves in the air in conditions neither is happy about, each one fervently wishing that the other would make the obviously sensible decision. You should try very hard never to allow another pilot, or business superior, or even an air traffic controller, pressure you into flying beyond what you honestly know are your own personal limitations.

Limitations also depend on other circumstances. Will it be necessary to come back later the same day or is the return open-ended? Are you happy about the conditions whilst you are flying this particular aeroplane? How flexible are your schedules? Geography also has a bearing on the question. What might be perfectly acceptable weather for a trip to a well known destination, may be very marginal for one you have never seen before. Low cloud cover over flat land in East Anglia or Denmark is a very different creature from low cloud cover in the mountainous country of Scotland or Switzerland. What may be acceptable in your home environment could be very much more difficult to cope with as a stranger in a foreign land.

When considering the question of weather limitations (as in many other aspects of flying) one of the best maxims I know is; always keep your options open. There is nothing worse than finding yourself totally committed to getting through to the only available landing place when the conditions there are marginal, to say the least. It isn't only IFR pilots who need alternates. You should always leave yourself with at least one alternative route and destination, in case conditions deteriorate or an emergency occurs. Never leave yourself without an 'out'.

First Find Your Forecast

Once upon a time (and to pilots who have recently arrived upon the scene this may very well sound just like a fairy story) every aerodrome of any size had a met forecaster on duty. If you were flying from one of those that did not, you could telephone (at normal phone prices) to the nearest aerodrome (civil or military) with a met section, to the local met office or weather centre, and have a chat with a forecaster there about the conditions you were likely to meet in the area where you were planning to fly. Phone the day before and they would prepare a comprehensive route forecast for you, METARs, TAFs, synoptic charts and all the rest. It was all part of the service, and even if the accuracy of some of the forecasts for more than the next hour or two was sometimes of doubtful accuracy, it was a great deal better and safer than the service available to pilots today. You learned as time went on how some forecasters were somewhat optimistic, tending to tell you what they thought you, as a VFR pilot, wanted to hear. You soon learned to distrust those to some extent. You came across the perpetual pessimists too; if you followed their dire prognostications about fog possibly coming in early, the chance of thunderstorms building up, the probability that the warm front would stall and hang around for days, then you would hardly ever have got off the ground at all.

I well remember the days when Birmingham Airport had a manned met office with forecasters at the disposal of all pilots. One afternoon I was there receiving a long and involved briefing from a forecaster for my proposed flight from Birmingham to Belgium. I cogitated over his advice, picked up the TAFs, METARs and synoptic charts, and thanked him for the information. As I was about to leave the office the Captain of a British European Airways Vanguard came across and quietly said, 'You know, old chap, you almost sounded as though you believed what that long-winded bugger was telling you there'. Like most pilots who have experienced a personal forecast, I must admit I always have preferred that to anything that appears on a PC or Minitel screen, is heard on an automated phone system or spews out of a fax machine.

Forecasting has, however, during the 1980s and '90s, become much more precise, with sophisticated computer programs crunching data from all over the globe and producing fairly accurate forecasts for several days ahead. These do go wrong occasionally but in general you can be reasonably sure that an eight-hour TAF will not be too far off the mark these days. Just the same, it does pay any pilot to keep in mind a couple of little realised facts about TAFs and METARs. A METAR is a report; it was probably absolutely accurate when prepared, but it is history by the time you read it. A TAF is no more than a forecast; it is, at best, an educated guesstimate by some so-called expert, which indicates what weather he or she believes is likely to occur in the coming hours. Mentioning expert forecasters takes me back to Colorado, where the US Weather Bureau once had to ask a Denver newspaper to stop publishing a very popular personal weekly weather forecast that appeared alongside their official one. The popular one, which more often than not turned out to be far more accurate than its professional counterpart, was produced by a 90-year-old who based his forecast on how the wound he got during World War I was feeling that particular week.

Weather Safety at a Price

However, even if the METAR is brand new and the TAFs are accurate ones, there is still trouble for the poor pilot. Unless you fly from a major aerodrome where they have all the data available (or, even better, the computer equipment to call the latest up for you) the private pilot flying VFR (for whom weather information is far more important than for the average instrument rated airline pilot) has to get hold of this vital information independently. In Britain, the Met Office has been forced to start charging for aviation met, whether this is accessed by telephone, fax or by one of the more sophisticated systems such as the Met Office's PC-based MIST. Premium rate phone numbers, deliberately slow-speed fax polling and expensive connection charges all push up the price of this vital safety information. It can become a seriously expensive business to obtain actuals, forecasts and charts covering a couple of hours flight from say the north of England to the Channel Islands or to the Orkneys perhaps. The Air Navigation Order makes it mandatory for the commander of any aircraft registered in the United Kingdom to:

> *reasonably satisfy himself before the aircraft takes off that the flight can safely be made, taking into account the latest information available as to ... the weather reports and forecasts available and any alternative course of action that can be adopted in case the flight cannot be completed as planned.*

(ANO No2 Order 1995, Article 38a)

Up to date forecasts and reports can be obtained from other sources than the Met Office however, and high UK costs have led to some pilots accessing the German or French weather fax services, which provide the data on normal-rate phone lines, which often work out less expensive than the Met Office's premium-rate lines. The Internet also is a useful and inexpensive source of TAFs and METARs, satellite images and synoptic charts, for the increasing number of pilots who have access to it. It is important, however, to understand what is being downloaded here. Much of the data originates from the Met Office but reaches UK net-surfers via America and may be a little out of date. The satellite photographs also can be confusing, if not downright misleading, to anyone who has no experience of interpreting them. Private pilots are not expected to be qualified met forecasters, but the more background you can acquire in this direction, the better you will be placed to get the most out of met sources like these.

Newspaper weather charts are next door to useless, being based on information from many hours earlier, but some television forecasts can give pilots a reasonable idea of whether the weather is likely to be acceptable VMC or not. In the United States there is a dedicated satellite TV weather channel, with special aviation slots throughout the day, and at the time this book is being written there appears to be a possibility that this channel will shortly also become available on this side of the Atlantic, either on cable or on satellite. In the States this channel is running all day on TV sets at many FBOs and flying schools and it can be extremely useful to pilots. In the USA they also provide, instead of the UK's premium-rate phone to an automated answering machine, a free phone number that connects you with a real live fore-caster who is prepared to discuss with you in detail the weather along your proposed flight track.

A glance at a piece of seaweed hanging on a hook, or a crafty tap on a household barometer and a look across the airfield to assess the visibility, is perhaps sufficient for a few circuits or a short trip in the immediate vicinity of the home airfield. For anything more than that, all sensible pilots must brief themselves on the weather situation by one means or another. It isn't just a legal requirement; it is an eminently sensible safeguard against being caught out in conditions beyond your limitations. But in the end don't forget that all METARs are snapshots of what things were like at a given time in the past and TAFs are no more than one person's idea of what the future might hold. Use them for guidance; don't ever be so naive as to take them for gospel truth.

Marginal VFR

One of the most common situations in which PPL pilots flying VFR can sometimes get into serious trouble is when they find themselves without any reliable visual reference; they can consequently lose control of the aeroplane. This can happen to you while night flying, for instance if you unexpectedly fly into a cloud which can be virtually invisible to you in the darkness. It can also happen even in broad daylight and miles away from any cloud, if visibility drops too far. Other situations occur where pilots retain full control over their aircraft but end up flying into the ground, hills or other obstructions, for the simple reason that they cannot see them in time to avoid them. Outside controlled airspace in the UK you, as a PPL qualified pilot without an IMC rating, may legally fly VFR in visibilities down to three kilometres; this means you can see no farther than objects which are just 48 seconds flying time ahead of you at 120 knots ground speed... and a lot less if you happen to be flying something as slick as a Bonanza. Not a great deal of time to see and avoid, but for an alert pilot, probably adequate.

The serious problems begin to rear their ugly heads when conditions deteriorate below the VMC limitations. It is illegal to continue flight into such conditions but regardless of this, it can and does happen, for various reasons (including the reason that you may have had a forecast for good VMC all the way but it has turned out to be over-optimistic). It is a fact that, even if the general visibility is at or just above the VFR limit of 3,000 metres, there are going to be some places where it thickens up to well under that magic figure. A general overcast cloud base of 1,200 feet may well seem fine for a VFR trip, except that cloud bases are not always perfectly flat and can dip down uncomfortably in places, perhaps in the very places where the topography of the land tilts up, just to make your marginal VFR even more marginal. Flying towards a frontal system can sometimes result in your finding yourself in deteriorating weather conditions that have already closed in behind you, whilst over terrain that gives little option for a precautionary landing. Foolishly pushing things to the limits like that can end up with you finding yourself well and truly stuck in marginal weather conditions. Just where you draw your own margin is largely a matter of personal choice. For some pilots it is quite a long way above the official limits for VFR. Others may well be prepared to chance their arms right down to the official minima. No private pilot, however experienced, should take it one iota farther than that.

At one stage of aviation, before instrument flying became a serious possibility for light aircraft pilots, and before all the big improvements in radio and navigation equipment during the 1950s, virtually all GA weather flying was done under VFR. Pressing on under a lowering cloud base and deteriorating visibility was known as 'scud running' and you had to have some prowess as a scud runner to have any kudos in certain flying circles. But back in these days there were very few 1,000 foot TV aerials, no mobile phone masts and much less regulated airspace to worry about. Aircraft tended to be slower too, yet despite that, scud running occasionally scared the pilots silly and not all that infrequently killed them. It still does. Accident reports continue to give as causes contributing to (frequently fatal) accidents such things as 'continued VFR flight into IMC' and 'controlled flight into terrain'. It is sad that there are still so many pilots who believe that licence limitations, flight rules and the rest, only apply to other people and not to themselves.

The best way of coping with marginal VFR is to adopt a few sensible tactics aimed at keeping you out of it. The object of a cross-country flight is to get to the destination, but a good tactical pilot knows that it is even more important to be around to get there another day if conditions militate against it on the first attempt. Of paramount importance on a marginal day is a good flight plan. Planning a VFR trip in marginal conditions is a good deal more critical than planning a similar flight under IFR. It is essential to plan the route in such a way that you will continuously have a close idea of where you are. A GPS moving map is fine, but don't blindly put your life in its hands. Plan your route to avoid natural obstructions like mountains, remembering that what is called orographic lifting can cause the cloud base to be considerably lower around mountains and high ground than elsewhere. Make it your aim to track alongside unmistakable line features as far as possible. Keep a finger on the paper chart all the way, replicating the job of the symbol on the moving map. Your chart is much more precise for features like coastline shape, it shows all the roads and railways and has all the obstructions marked on it, which is more than you can say for most GPS moving maps. Just the same, having a GPS running as back-up can be invaluable, especially if the marginal weather reaches your bottom line and you want to use its 'nearest airfields' feature to beat a quick and safe retreat.

Sooner is Better than Later

It is important never to delay that retreat too long. A shower of rain ahead can often engender the feeling that you will pass through it in a couple of minutes and things will be fine again on the other side. But a shower of rain in marginal conditions means the visibility is bound to be significantly reduced, and probably means that the cloud base will be lower as well. Betting your life on an improvement on the other side is not good tactics. It is tempting providence. As you fly into such conditions you may well be forced lower to stay clear of cloud; this brings you into the danger area for collision with hills or obstructions you may only be able to see when it is too late to avoid them. The bad tactician, or the pilot whose flight plan has gone awry, is liable at this stage to panic, slam on power and pull the nose up trying to find a safe altitude. This is the stage where loss of control is quite likely to come into the equation. Even instrument rated pilots, who are in practice with their instrument flying, can find an unpremeditated transition from VFR into IMC like this very tricky to cope with. So what chances does the average private pilot have, with only rudimentary instrument training, or even the IMC rated pilot who is out of instrument flying practice?

When marginal weather conditions are around you will perhaps come across a pilot who poo-poos the whole thing and tries to persuade you that forecasts are always pessimistic. He knows the area well and tells you that just like him (it seldom is a her) you'll be able to make it okay. Peer pressure can sometimes be very difficult to resist, but if you believe your best tactic is to stay on *terra firma* then have the courage of your own convictions, not the bravado of his. And if you do take off, only to find that your adviser was (as you probably expected anyway) totally mistaken, then don't continue flying into conditions you are unhappy about. Flying should be an enjoyable activity. It really is a shame to use it simply to scare yourself and your passengers silly.

Advice about Ice

By the time many pilots have ceased to be students and have at last qualified for their PPLs, they have developed an almost morbid fear of ice. It is admittedly quite nice stuff to have in a gin and tonic, perhaps bearable in a carburetter since there is a pretty straightforward and well-known way of getting rid of it from there, but pilots find positively terrifying the thought of ice becoming involved with aeroplanes in any other way. The very word 'Icing' seems to have a chilling effect on them. This pathological fear of ice arises simply because all text books on aviation meteorology and airmanship carefully warn pilots over and over again of the dangers of airframe icing. Flying instructors then assiduously re-emphasise these solemn warnings in such a way that no student pilot can ever be unaware of the ice hazard, which, like an evil spirit, is constantly lurking just around the corner. It is no small wonder that many pilots end up in such awe of icing that they refuse to take to the air at any time when the temperature is anywhere near, never mind below, freezing. As for planning a flight at or above the forecast freezing level, many pilots regard that as tantamount to attempted suicide.

A healthy respect for airframe icing is of course essential if you want to enjoy a long life and still like flying little aeroplanes. On the other hand the exaggerated level of dread of ice that many instructors, and a lot of flying training manuals, instill into student pilots' minds does tend to put an unnecessary limitation on their future flying activities. The fact is that, as a private pilot without an IMC or instrument rating, all you have to do to remain clear of icing conditions is to stay within the limitations of your licence.

About the only forms of airframe icing you are ever likely to encounter if you stick to this rule are the kinds that occur whilst the aircraft is on the ground. This can take the form of hoar frost, that forms when an aircraft has been parked in the open on a clear night at temperatures of zero or below, or, very rarely, water that may have collected in the airframe (say at the bottom of a rudder or in an elevator where the drain hole is blocked) and then been frozen there. To ensure that your aircraft is airworthy it is of course essential to remove all of these forms of ice (together with any associated snow) before even thinking about taxying out to take off. Even thin layers of hoar frost can seriously reduce the aerodynamic efficiency of an aircraft, sometimes to the extent that take-off becomes impossible.

These forms of ice apart, it is only on very rare occasions that a law-abiding VFR pilot might encounter another type of airframe icing. This is generally known as rain ice. This can form on an aircraft whilst it is flying if the temperature of the aircraft is below freezing point and it happens to encounter a shower of rain. The raindrops are then liable to freeze immediately on contact with the cold aircraft. Alternatively, and again only very seldom in the UK, the same effect can also occur as freezing rain. On the very rare occasions that freezing rain is encountered, it is usually when rain from the clouds which are associated with a warm front falls through an inversion. These chilled raindrops will then freeze into a glasslike layer on the first thing they contact, be that telephone wires, power lines, road surfaces . . . or aeroplanes. Nasty stuff, presenting problems for almost all forms of transport. It is best avoided by pilots, either by staying on the ground when such conditions are forecast, or by flying straight back out of the rain, immediately it shows the first sign of forming ice on the airframe. Freezing rain, of course, actually makes up a bit for its nasty characteristics by frequently forming black ice on the roads, which makes it very difficult for the pilot to drive to the airfield in the first place.

Flying is Fine in Frosty Weather

The fact that the air temperature may be well below freezing does not by itself mean that anyone flying VFR is foolishly asking for trouble from icing. Airframe icing will normally occur only when the aircraft is actually flying in cloud or in very poor visibility conditions (both probably outside the VFR limitations of your private pilot licence). Supercooled droplets in the mist or clouds can then build up into layers of clear ice, rime ice or hoar frost on the aircraft surfaces.

Very few aircraft of the types flown by private pilots are fitted with any form of ice protection, other than pitot head heaters, and virtually none of them are cleared for flight into known icing conditions. So even if you have followed the advice given later (see Chapter 6) and gone ahead to qualify for an IMC or Instrument Rating, you would still be going outside legal limitations (this time those of the aircraft rather than your own licence and ratings) were you to fly into icing conditions of the type described.

It is unfortunately true that not every pilot invariably flies 100% within the letter of the law, and some might decide to exercise the privileges of their instrument rating by climbing through a layer of cloud where icing was forecast, simply in order to reach clear air above it. Or, because icing conditions tend to be somewhat erratic and unpredictable, you might be flying happily along in cloud where the temperature is well above freezing, when suddenly you see with dismay the OAT probe, some rivet heads and then the corners of the windshield gradually beginning to vanish under a rough white substance. The first time this happens, because of all the horror stories fed to you during your flying training, your immediate reaction will probably be one of horror. You just know that the aircraft is shortly going to look like one of the textbooks photographs which appear to show aeroplanes being swallowed up by glaciers. But what probably happens next is that (while you are working out whether it is safe, terrain-wise, to descend, or whether a 180 degree turn to rescue your aircraft from its imminent terminal dive will be accepted by ATC) you begin to realise that the machine is actually still flying, maintaining height and responding to the controls. It obviously has never read the textbooks about what it was supposed to do in icing conditions.

When you then realise that you are not about to die and that an aircraft can in fact carry a certain amount of ice accretion without falling like a brick out of the sky, you are liable to say to yourself that icing is no big deal, and to begin believing that all the warnings you were given as a student were just plumb stupid. This is the perfect way to begin a dangerously complacent attitude towards icing. You experienced a light, short-lived form of icing on this occasion, and were sensible enough to get the hell out of the area as soon as possible. Icing isn't always as bad as the warnings paint it, but it certainly isn't guaranteed always to be as easy to cope with as you had it this time.

The first, second and final lesson about icing and airborne aeroplanes that you should commit to memory is that time is of the essence. Every moment longer than necessary that you stay in icing conditions is a moment too long, a moment in which the windows become more opaque, the lifting surfaces lose more of their aerodynamic shape and efficiency, the weight of the aircraft increases. The sooner you get right out of there, the better for all concerned. Circumstances will dictate whether you should climb, descend or make a 180 and turn back; what you must never do is simply soldier on, hoping it will all go away like a bad dream.

If you ever should be unlucky enough to end up in charge of a really heavily iced aeroplane, you must be aware of the fact that it will almost certainly behave very differently from its normal self. With increased weight, disfigured aerofoil sections, opaque windshield and so on, you have to be ready for it to demonstrate decidedly unusual quirks as you try to bring it back in to land. With a modicum of luck, as you descend into warmer air most of the ice will melt away, but if there is freezing air all the way down to ground level you may not be so fortunate. Lowering the flaps on an iced-up aeroplane can also have highly unpredictable results and is generally highly inadvisable. This is so because the tailplane of a conventional aeroplane is designed to produce a down force to keep the machine stable in the air. But tailplanes have sharper leading edges than wings and ice tends to form most eagerly on sharp edges (just look at the OAT probe, antennae, rivet heads etc). So the necessary down force from the tail is probably already severely compromised by ice that is probably completely invisible to you from your seat in the cockpit, and lowering flaps can seriously aggravate that situation, making the aircraft distinctly liable to nose over sharply. Under these conditions it is better by far to pick an aerodrome with an adequately long runway and then come in to land flapless and at an appreciably higher than normal threshold speed, in consideration of the unknown altered aerodynamics and all the extra weight you may be carrying.

It is necessary for pilots to keep a reasonable sense of perspective about airframe icing, in exactly the same way as it is necessary to keep issues like getting lost on a cross-country or contending with engine failure in sensible proportion. Be alert to the possible dangers, but don't allow them to colour your whole attitude towards flying and, as a result, spoil your enjoyment of it.

Choking on Icicles

Carburetter icing is something else entirely. It is not necessarily associated with wintry temperatures; in fact it is really quite likely to raise its ugly head when the ambient temperature of the air is quite warm. Due to the effect of evaporation of the fuel and the reduction in the pressure of the air as it passes through the carburetter venturi, the temperature of this air can drop very considerably. If the air being sucked in by the engine happens to contain a lot of water vapour this can freeze inside the system. The gradual reduction of airflow caused by the formation of this ice can cause an insidious drop in engine performance. This can come on so gradually that an unwary pilot might not even notice it at first, and might simply nudge the throttle open a little to compensate for the loss of power. Quite soon the power will drop off a bit yet again and if the pilot doesn't get the message, the aircraft will soon find itself with the throttle fully open and the power still inexorably easing off. A reduction in revs on a fixed pitch propeller aircraft, or an unexplained drop in manifold pressure in an aircraft with a constant speed propeller, are signs that should never be ignored in that way. Carburetter icing is very easy to contend with if caught at an early stage of formation, but if the pilot ignores the build-up too long, then it can be a very different matter. The engine can eventually lose so much power that it is no longer generating the heat necessary to warm up the hot air that is the only way the pilot has of thawing out the ice in the carburetter. A vicious circle, indeed.

Every aircraft handbook has its section describing how best to handle carburetter icing and since these methods vary somewhat from one aircraft to another it is as well to know the system for each type that you are in the habit of flying. In general it is inadvisable ever to use partial carb heat as a preventive measure; this can actually encourage the formation of the ice that you are trying to avoid. Application of full hot air as soon as carburetter ice begins to form (or at other times as laid down for certain flight conditions or throttle settings) is what is normally called for. It is an action that can initially have some rather alarming consequences, as the engine begins to cough, snort, hesitate and run rough as it goes through the process of swallowing the water produced from the melting ice that has been the original cause of the power loss. Have faith however, and in a few moments the power will come back with a rush . . . and you will soon be made aware of all those nudges you gave to the throttle lever before you realised what it was that was really going on. Keep the full hot air applied until you get out of the conditions that caused the ice in the first place. If need be, adjust the mixture to compensate for the lower density of the hot air. If you remain alert to the possibility of carb icing occurring and follow the aircraft handbook advice, this should guarantee that you never have any more than the occasional, very short-lived, encounter with the often overdramatized bogeyman of carburetter ice.

Wonderful Weather for Flying

Most books about flying weather dwell (as I must admit I have done to some extent too) on all the nastier aspects of meteorology that can make flying uncomfortable, dangerous or just plain impossible. There is, however, another side to this weather question. Pilots who allow themselves to become purely 'fair weather flyers' really do let a great deal of enjoyable flying pass them by, getting into the air only on days when the visibility is for ever, the sky is an unblemished blue and the wind is warm, light and steady. There are lots of other types of weather which can make practising your prowess as a pilot a thoroughly enjoyable experience. Don't let your prejudices prevent you from making good use of all the days when these conditions prevail.

What About Winter?

Take winter for a start. You really shouldn't give up flying just because the weather happens to have turned a little chilly. There was a time when only a few hardy souls, and the masochists among us, went flying in freezing temperatures when we had nothing but little open cockpit aeroplanes to fly, but present-day light aircraft nearly all are fitted with some creature comforts like windscreens, draught-proofing and efficient heaters; the days of frostbitten fingers and icicles forming on handlebar moustaches, belong to the past. Crisp, clear, frosty weather can make for superb visibility. Navigating by map-reading over a snow covered landscape offers a whole new experience to any pilot who has never encountered that enchanting scene before. Believe me, when you have done it once you certainly will want to repeat the exercise. It can be quite exhilarating and can reveal facets of the countryside below that you will never have seen in warmer weather.

Generally Britain is not affected by extreme weather that turns engine oil into toffee, freezes greased controls solid, and makes engine preheating essential before flight. And even in regions like Alaska, Canada and Siberia, where extreme conditions do occur regularly, GA seldom comes to a grinding halt. Admittedly, even in the UK, never mind more arctic regions, you can end up with pretty numb fingertips after scraping hoar frost off the airframe surfaces before flying. Carrying out a thorough and careful preflight inspection in subzero temperatures also calls for a certain amount of stamina, perseverance and strength of character to stop you cutting the odd corner (such as kneeling down in the snow to inspect for water in the fuel system, perhaps) but it can all certainly be well worth the effort involved. The sky can be a wonderful place on a bitterly cold winter day, after the early morning mist that often follows a clear frosty night has burned off from the white landscape. Winter sunshine is weak and causes few thermals, so flying is much smoother than on a warm summer day. It's the ideal time to fly your air-sickness susceptible aunt, perhaps. Polar air tends to be free from industrial pollution and so visibility can be superb. Another winter plus point is that the sky is much emptier; less circuit traffic means more air time per hour. The RT frequencies are quieter and the whole sky is usually a lot more peaceful. Flying is much more relaxed than when you have to share the sky with everybody else on a busy summer afternoon. Winter scenery from the air can also be magnificent, especially in and around mountains; it is totally different from other times of the year. Night flying can be blissful too; clear hard frost with sparkling streetlights below and an ocean of stars above. All the pilots who lock up their logbooks and licences for the winter really don't know the sheer enjoyment they are missing.

Even the aeroplane seems to like winter flying. The higher density of cold air packs more energy into each engine cylinder than on a hot summer day, and so you actually have a marginally higher-performance machine to fly. Its range is, in theory, slightly greater too, since cold fuel is also denser than warm fuel; as a result each tank carries a little more weight of fuel when full and it is the weight of fuel on board, rather than the volume, that determines the range of an aircraft.

Looking over my own early logbooks I see that I averaged more hours between November and February in the first few years of my flying career than I ever did between May and July. Much of that flying was done in Scotland . . . and in open-cockpit aircraft too. Yet, in retrospect at least, it was mainly thoroughly enjoyable flying, of which I have many fond memories. Given due respect for the prevailing conditions, winter can often offer flying that is every bit as much fun as in other seasons. Many pilots actually prefer winter flying, despite its occasional drawbacks and difficulties.

Even Fog can be Beautiful

Fog is not a weather phenomenon that encourages many pilots to rush into the air. It can be downright dangerous to any non-instrument rated pilot of a light aircraft and yet, given the right conditions, it can occasionally provide pilots with an enchanting experience. When river fog is creeping slowly up a valley and spilling over the adjacent hills to blanket the countryside all around, the pilot's eye view gives a marvellous insight into the workings of mother nature and brings alive the pages of meteorology textbooks. Of course, if your home airfield happens to lie in the line of approach of this blanket of fog, you would be better not to prolong this practical weather study course to the point where a safe return to base becomes too touch-and-go. Occasionally too, after early morning fog has cleared from your base airfield sufficiently to permit flying under VFR, there may still be areas of it lingering in the vicinity, turning the usual workaday landscape into something almost etherial. Lines of electricity pylons stride across an invisible landscape; the rippling light grey shroud covering the fields is broken only by occasional church towers, chimneys, rows of trees or areas of upland. Whether such flying is quite legal VFR is open to question; are you really 'in sight of the surface'? On the other hand, in the remote contingency of an engine failure under these conditions, you are surely in no more dangerous a situation than you would be were the same thing to occur during night flying or an over water transit. You can certainly enjoy this mystic scene of mist below you in safety, even in a single engine aeroplane, by keeping close to the boundary of the foggy area and remembering how quickly some types of fog can roll in.

The one way you should never plan to view a layer of shallow fog from above is when it is forecast to clear from your destination aerodrome before the time you expect to get there. It may look quite pretty thirty miles out but it begins to look more nasty than pretty if you get closer and find it hasn't obeyed the forecast. The clearance of this type of fog is notoriously difficult for forecasters to predict and it is best never to rely on forecast clearance times. Under these circumstances, either wait where you are until you get a METAR from the destination confirming that it is clear of fog, or carry a adequate fuel reserve to allow for diversion to an aerodrome that you know is clear, and forecast to remain clear. Don't be caught out by local quirks of climate and topography either. Just because an aerodrome near to your destination is reporting clear of fog, it doesn't necessarily mean that the one you are heading for is also clear. Quite insignificant differences in height or nearness to water or hills for example, can make all the difference to the formation and clearance of advection fog, radiation fog and mist.

Not Getting the Wind up

Wind tends to put many pilots off flying, especially if it is blowing at anything approaching right-angles to the runway. You never know just when that is liable to be the very situation you find yourself in on arrival at a airfield one day, and so crosswind landings are something you should practice rather than treat like the plague and try always to avoid. The art of achieving a satisfactory crosswind landing is one that brings a considerable degree of smug satisfaction even to old hands at the game. If you had an instructor who tended to postpone the lesson every time the wind was being awkward, you owe it to yourself to find another instructor who is willing to help you master this gentle art. There are aficionados of the one-wing-low system and other pilots who swear by the crabbing approach. Some aeroplane types and some pilots seem to be more suited to one than the other but neither is wrong, so if you find the one your mentor is trying to teach you feels uncomfortable or is giving you a hard time, try the other one. Once you have mastered your chosen technique and feel you can handle a crosswind up to something approaching the aircraft handbook's maximum demonstrated crosswind figure, the sting should have vanished from crosswinds. A small refinement you might like to add to crosswind techniques, under appropriate circumstances, is to break with the habits of a lifetime and ignore the white line down the centre of the runway. If the crosswind is strong, your take-off or landing roll will be short, and if the runway involved is a reasonably broad one the simple expedient of starting the take-off, or touching down, in one corner, heading as much into the crosswind as possible, can pay dividends. If you have a 25 knot wind that is 40 off the runway heading you are contending with about 16 knots of crosswind component; slew at least the initial part of your landing/take-off roll by even 10° into wind and the crosswind you have to wrestle with has dropped to just 12 knots. It can make an appreciable difference, but does need a bit of practice too. And that is another reason for not being shy about flying on windy days.

Brighten Up a Day

The sky is leaden; a layer of stratus hangs over the airfield and seems to stretch to infinity. Not much of a day for flying, is it? And yet, even on a dull looking day like this, the weather has several flying plus points. The air is pretty stable and free from thermal turbulence, so provided the cloud base is acceptably high and precipitation isn't affecting visibility too much, it can be not a bad day for a bit of circuit practice, or for taking someone with a susceptible stomach up for a smooth little flight. Also, since this type of cloud usually indicates settled weather, if you don't make use of it, you are quite possibly going to have to wait rather a long time for anything better to come along.

Don't Let Rain Stop Play

The TV weather map is covered with these black clouds with rain symbols below them and half suns peeping out above them. If it's going to be rainy then there's no point in flying, is there? If you were to adopt that as a firm philosophy then, certainly so long as you are based in the United Kingdom (or in much of the rest of Europe for that matter) you would find yourself being very severely restricted in your flying activities. Refusing to fly any time there is a chance of the aircraft going through the airborne equivalent of a free car wash, does very considerably cut down on a pilot's flying activity. As mentioned elsewhere, the torrential rain associated with cumulonimbus thunderstorm clouds is something you must avoid at all costs, but the steady drizzle from reasonably high nimbostratus, or the short sharp showers from ordinary cumulus clouds are relatively innocuous to aircraft. You can usually avoid isolated showers of rain in order to maintain better visibility, but areas of light rain are not normally the cause of drastic reductions in visibility. Admittedly, heavy drizzle does tend to go along with high humidity and visibility down to under 3,000 metres. Rainwater also blows off the windshield of a light aircraft without any appreciable restriction to the pilot's vision. (That is one reason why the manufacturers don't bother to fit them with windscreen wipers.) If the rain happens to be associated with an approaching frontal system with steadily lowering cloud base, deteriorating visibility and worsening weather, then any thoughts of flying should be reconsidered and VFR flying might well be inadvisable. So far as isolated showers are concerned, those typical of the cold sector after a front has passed through are just one of the features of what is actually a chunk of sky that can make for really pleasant flying conditions.

Snow showers are somewhat different. For a start, even moderate snow has a drastic effect on visibility from an aircraft, and you are unlikely to be able to maintain VMC whilst flying in anything more than very light snow. Dry snow normally flutters harmlessly past aircraft without causing any airframe icing, but flight in sleet or wet snow can result in air filters and engine air intakes becoming blocked by ice accretions. Since virtually no light aircraft are cleared for flight in known icing conditions, simply obeying these aircraft limitations should keep you clear of this hazard.

Inclement Weather can make Flying Fun

It always seems a pity when people who you feel should really be enterprising pilots turn into dyed-in-the-wool fair weather flyers. By spurning the challenges and fulfilment of flying competently through a bit of precipitation and around a few clouds, and avoiding subzero temperatures or stiff crosswinds, they deny themselves a great deal of what flying has to offer. The obvious end result of this is that these pilots are never really able to make full use of their licences. Except in extremely favourable weather situations (more often to be found in places like South Africa or California than in western Europe) they will always be reluctant to undertake anything more than local flights, and will miss out on much of the potential that a pilot's licence should bring with it. Don't restrict your flying like that. Accepting the occasional weather challenge and seeing the sky in many of its moods, benign or otherwise, is all part and parcel of being a pilot.

It is only by experiencing different sorts of weather that a pilot can come to understand it. Pretty pictures and neat diagrams in textbooks are all very well, but only by flying through something a bit more interesting than clear blue summer skies will you come to understand the element in which you are going to spend the flying hours of your life. Feel the wind under your wings on a blustery day. Learn to enjoy the sensation of flying through rain showers the way you used to enjoy splashing through puddles as a kid. Find out what it is like to fly on a frosty winter night with black overcast above you and fairyland city lights below. Provided you accept your own limitations and those of the aircraft you are using, and provided you fly consistently within them, this type of flying should never expose you to any unacceptable risk. It will, on the other hand, enable you to do so much more with your licence, add so much to your experience of airmanship, enable you to pilot the aircraft on visits to more places and generally add to your overall enjoyment of being a pilot. If you opt out of this challenge and stick in the unexciting rut of the 'fair weather flyer', you will never experience the wonderment of seeing the silhouette of your aircraft in the centre of a multicoloured, perfectly circular rainbow against the clouds, or enjoy the magic of watching a full moon rise above a broken layer of stratus, or experience the joy of chasing medullary rays like celestial searchlights from above.

Chapter 4

Different Environments

No Angst about Airports

If you are a newly fledged pilot who has done virtually all of your training at a small airfield or even at a quietish regional airport, the idea of flying in for the first time to a busy international airport can take on the guise of quite an adventure. A quick look at *Pooley's Guide* or the *UK VFR Flight Guide* will soon confirm your suspicions that coping with the traffic and controllers there, is likely to be a whole new ball-game compared with what you have considered normal circuit procedure up till now. It is, but, like many other aspects of flying, all that is really needed to get rid of any anxiety you feel is a clear understanding of what is actually involved. Remember, if you had been trained at a flying club or school based at, for example, Manchester International, Glasgow or Birmingham airports, you would probably be just as anxious about your first attempt to carry out an overhead join at a grass aerodrome with only a ground/air radio instead of full ATC service.

The very diversity of the aerodromes that are available for you to use is one of the major advantages of flying as a GA pilot. To rule any category of these out of your plans for future flying would be to cut off your nose to spite your face, as the old saying goes. Within my own first fifty hours of flying I had visited only a meagre eight airfields, each of which was fairly small and the busiest of which was Fairoaks. (At least Fairoaks is still active; of the others I used in those days, Portsmouth, Hamble and Ouston are no more, and the future of a couple of the others seems to be hanging in the balance.) My logbooks now show take-offs and landings at well over 500 airports, airfields, landing grounds and strips, many of which conjure up special memories and meanings for me.

It is quite marvellous how so many aerodromes have managed to retain a special character of their own, despite the stereotyping that has occurred at most of the major ones. The need for security has led to the disappearance or sanitization of such things as airport visitors' galleries. Even non-flyers used to share in some of the excitement of aviation there with their cameras and binoculars, bringing an ambience to the airport that no contingent of 'reggie-spotters' ever can. Unfortunately many of the smaller airfields too are now full of fencing, security barriers, no entry signs and policed doorways leading to airside. All of this is sadly necessary, just a sign of the times in which we live, but it certainly does detract from the atmosphere our aerodromes used to have. Some of them have still managed to preserve something of their character though, despite what has been foisted upon them by contemporary circumstances.

Airfields Worth Exploring

Some airfields are interesting to visit. In Britain, for instance, we are lucky still to have places like Barton. This was once Manchester's main airport and so decades of aviation history mingle here with present-day enthusiasm for light aviation; flying clubs, home-builders, young and old, airmen and women all congregate here. The access by air may be cramped under Manchester TMA, the runways are not over long by current standards and the grass does get a bit muddy in wet weather, but I always find the atmosphere thoroughly enjoyable. Yorkshire has a near equivalent to Lancashire's Barton too; Sherburn-in-Elmet. Sherburn has several grass runways which means that it is always possible to find one that is more or less into wind (but don't be tempted to use what looks like a vast concrete runway alongside; it isn't a runway any more). Again, here you will meet a real grass-roots enthusiasm, a touch of WW2 nostalgia in places and, just like Barton, you can generally be sure of a good honest bite to eat. Glenforsa in Mull is another marvellous airfield. A level grass runway lying betwixt the purple mountains and the sparkling sea with a fully functioning hotel/restaurant within a few paces of the field. Walking, angling, mountaineering and sight-seeing are all available practically on the spot. Another island airfield I always enjoy is Texel in the Netherlands; call the Tower 20 minutes out and they'll have your overnight B & B arranged and a hire car or bicycle waiting for you by the time you have parked the aircraft.

At the other end of the scale I have many fond memories of some very large and busy airports too. Among this category within the UK I give Birmingham, Newcastle, Glasgow and Norwich high praise for the efficiency of their handling and the general facilities they make available for pilots of small aircraft. Unfortunately, the same cannot be said about the costs involved in a flying visit to some of these larger aerodromes. Once you add up all the relevant landing, parking, handling and navigation charges it can set you back quite a bit. They could perhaps take a leaf out of the books of much bigger and busier places elsewhere in the world. Some years ago I was astounded by the comparatively low charges made by Frankfurt and Amsterdam (Schiphol), for the excellent service they gave me in slotting my relatively slow four-seat piston single, into their hectic traffic stream of jet airliners and then making room for it to park on the GA Apron. Their costs have risen somewhat since then, but at least they still make room for GA visitors, which is more than can be said for some airports not a million miles from the UK capital, where light aircraft are either not accepted at all or may reluctantly be offered a slot but at absolutely prohibitive charges. If you are considering getting in some practice in big airport procedures I would certainly not advise you to pick Heathrow, Gatwick or even Stansted for that exercise. Nor Munich's new airport where similar regimes exist, despite the fact that other German airports like Berlin (Schönefeld) Nuremberg, Stuttgart and Düsseldorf still remain reasonably user-friendly towards light aircraft.

I have flown small Cessnas, Pipers and Grummans in and out of many big airports in the United States, places such as Atlanta, Nashville, San Jose and Memphis, and I have seen there how light aircraft can be incorporated into the traffic pattern with no more than a reasonable bit of savvy and co-operation between Air Traffic Control and the pilots involved. In most of the United States and in many other countries it appears to be an accepted part of aviation that international airliners, commuter flights, business and private aircraft can, and do, share the same airport facilities.

Private Pilots Play Their Part

For smooth integration to take place at major airports of course the pilots involved must be on top of their jobs, none more so than the light aircraft jockeys whose mounts are appreciably slower than the majority of users. Busy controllers have little time to spare for 'say again' requests from private pilots who have been unable to anticipate what the next call was likely to be. Nor do they welcome long-winded pilots whose RT transmissions take up too much airtime. Quick, alert, clear and concise transmissions are what is wanted here. It may all sound pretty bewildering on first acquaintance (which is one good reason for having an instructor or a more experienced fellow pilot along on a first trip into such an airport) but it soon falls into place and becomes almost second nature. It really does; even to the pilot who was brought up in the more casual surroundings of 'Little Grassfield on the Hump'.

Some pilots from places like Little Grassfield are in considerable awe of 'real' airports with Approach, Tower and maybe Radar and Ground control, Automated Terminal Information Service (ATIS) and the rest. They feel scared of making a botch of things and having their performance reported to the CAA. But ATC is not there to write tickets. Their aim is simply to keep their traffic flowing safely and efficiently; your aim should be to co-operate in helping them achieve this. If your inexperience does occasion a minor slip, ATC are almost invariably prepared to turn a blind eye, provided you are honest with them. To avoid making such minor errors, the best thing to do is to emulate the Boy Scouts, and 'be prepared'. As mentioned in Chapter 2, if you have the chance to do so, listening to airport RT procedures on a hand-held or scanner receiver can be a big help in preparing yourself. It gets you familiar with the sequence of instructions, the phraseology used and the conciseness expected of you, long before you actually fly into the area. In many cases ATC actually makes flying a lot easier for you than it is when you are operating from a smaller airfield. Your first task, if the airport has an ATIS frequency is to listen to it and make a note of the information it gives you. Then when you call the initial contact frequency, tell them you have 'Information Kilo' or whatever its code letter was at the time. In America, even when there is no ATIS broadcast, some pilots say every airfield still does have its ATIS; by listening out on Tower frequency you can glean in advance from ATC conversations with other aircraft which runway is in use, what the wind is, QNH, QFE and any significant weather factors. In the States, saying you 'have the numbers' as part of your initial 'who you are, where you are and what you want to do' contact, sometimes allows the controller to save time and breath; it seldom seems to work that way here in UK.

If you have a transponder on board, don't forget to let ATC know; it can make life a lot simpler for you and for them if you are allocated a code to squawk so that they can identify you positively on their radar screens. Radar or Approach will feed you instructions to manoeuvre you into a suitable position relative to the runway and to other traffic, then Tower is likely to slot you into a gap in the landing sequence without you having to make any effort on your own. You will, as often as not, be allowed to approach the airport direct from your present position, either on a straight-in approach or onto right or left base. It does make life a lot easier for you than the procedure to which you are better accustomed; being locked into standard overhead joins and full circuits at uncontrolled airfields. All that is required of you at the bigger airport is to acknowledge the instructions and do precisely what you have been told to do. The more conversant you become with ATC procedures, the easier it all becomes. Occasionally it is only after you roll towards a stop on the runway that you find your troubles really beginning. At places like this you don't simply backtrack to the one and only exit from the runway; you will probably be told something like 'Take the third exit on your left and contact Ground on 121.35' after which Ground are quite likely to come up with a series of instructions about 'Link Charlie, taxiways Golf, Juliett and Mike, North Apron and Stand 38' or other things of that nature. If your *VFR Flight Guide* does have an airport diagram page with all that guff on it, do have it open and ready for action. If it doesn't, then do try, before you set out, to photocopy or borrow the appropriate page from someone who has an *Aerad* or *Jeppesen IFR Guide*. Without an airport diagram you can be up the creek without the proverbial paddle, annoying Ground Control who will then have to give you a long series of 'Next left' and 'Second on the right now' instructions to help you find your parking place. Which doesn't make you exactly the flavour of the month with them.

Conversion Course for Uncontrolled Airfields

The other side of the coin is the pilot who is familiar with flying at an ATC controlled aerodrome and yet pretty green about how to get in to one of these odd places where voices that seem to be masquerading as controllers say odd things like 'Land at your discretion' instead of giving you a normal clearance. Exercising your discretion is after all more difficult than simply obeying instructions, isn't it? As I said above, major airports can in some ways be easier for you to fly in to than small airfields. Where full ATC service is not provided you may encounter either Flight Information Service (call sign 'Information') or aerodrome Air/Ground Communication Service (call sign 'Radio') or you may find yourself at an airfield or airstrip with no RT service whatsoever. The idea of unregulated persons operating the ground end of the radio, or the very thought of landing at a place where there is nobody at all to talk to, fills some big airport trained pilots with considerable apprehension. Before you let that feeling build up too strongly, it is as well to remember that it wasn't all that long ago that very few light aircraft carried any radio at all, and that many of these small airfields and airstrips all around the country handle thousands of aircraft movements every year with minimal or no RT contact at all.

Wherever you trained, you will have learned the basic aerodrome circuit (or 'pattern', for any readers who did their training in the States). It is this simple circuit that forms the basis of flying in to these smaller airfields and strips. If you managed to achieve your PPL without making a non-radio approach and landing then I would suggest your instructor was a little remiss; you should get that omission rectified. Ask for an explanation of a standard overhead join, dead side descent and circuit procedure followed by a practical demonstration. It may initially seem odd compared with what you may be accustomed to. You do admittedly have to make an occasional decision yourself which ATC may up till now have been making for you, but there is no great mystery or magic involved. Where there is nobody watching from the tower or following your blip on a radar screen, it is up to you even more than usual to keep your eyes peeled for other traffic and to maintain your own separation from it. Working out from signal squares and windsocks which runway is in use, circuit direction, wind direction and strength all by yourself without ATC to tell you, is perhaps a new experience for you, but aviation lived that way quite happily for years before radio came along to make us all a bit lazier and less observant. Where the airfield has a radio frequency, even if this is unmanned, it is often a useful practice to listen for and to make calls known as 'traffic advisories', but these do not necessarily paint a complete traffic picture; there may be other aircraft around flying non-radio. Once you have got the hang of this type of operation in UK there may be a surprise waiting for you when you venture abroad. Circuit procedures, joining especially, can be very different in other European countries, despite JAR and all that. A flying visit to the United States will bring you into contact with the joys and jumbled radio calls of the Unicom system. There is more about that subject later in this Chapter.

Going to Grass

With the steady increases in the cost of operating aircraft from licensed aerodromes, landing, parking and hangar charges, there has been a steady increase in the use of small grass strips in the UK. We still have a long way to go before we reach the situation in the USA where there are somewhere around 15,000 active aerodromes, of which approximately 10,000 can be classified as grass strips or fields. Or to express that more correctly, they are unpaved; some may not be grass, but gravel, cinders, sand or just trodden earth. In the UK most (with the exception of Barra's runways which are of beach sand) at least purport to be grass, although some come pretty close to being just plain dirt at certain times of the year. Before heading off to make your first flight in to one of these little airfields, you would be well advised to have someone experienced in strip flying come with you and show you the rudiments of the game. Most of these fields are fairly short, so a thorough revision of your short field techniques would not come amiss, especially if you have reached that big airport frame of mind where you now regard anything less than 2,000 metres as a short field. It is also essential to learn all you can about your proposed destination, from *Pooley's* or the *Lockyear Farm Strip Guide* perhaps. Virtually all of these places are private property, and it is only polite, as well as being a requirement, to phone the owners in advance to notify them of your intention to pay the place a visit. This is also an excellent time to find out the up to date situation and the condition of the field or strip. Are cattle grazing; is the field soft; is it open; has anybody perhaps put up a transmitter mast on the approach or telephone wires just off the threshold since your guide was printed? These things happen and it is much better to know about them before you get there. That is one of the purposes of the Prior Permission Requirement (PPR).

Grass requires you to adopt a rather different landing and take-off style compared with hard-surface runways, especially if the surface is rough or undulating. Tailwheel aircraft in general fare better than tricycle undercarriage aircraft on grass but, provided you ease the loads on the nose-gear, even the latter can be flown perfectly safely and successfully from grass. I know of an American owner who regularly operates his Learjet from one. Grass strips are often a lot closer to where you want to fly than the nearest licensed aerodrome and if you are prepared to treat them with a little respect and use good judgement, there is no reason why you shouldn't include the suitable grass strips in your list of destinations. However, they have an unfortunate tendency to camouflage themselves into the background, looking like just one green field among so many others, so accurate navigation is often needed to find them. GPS can be an invaluable help to you here in picking out the correct field quickly. Once you have found your landing strip though, set up a well-judged approach and wait for that exhilarating feeling of dropping gently down onto nature's greensward with scarcely a sound from the tyres; that's so much nicer than the usual squeal of expensive rubber being rasped off by asphalt runways.

Most grass strips in the UK have single runways although a few, such as Ashcroft in Cheshire, Church Farm, near Banbury and Little Gransden near St Neots, do offer a choice of grass runways. Runway lengths vary, but only occasionally are they long enough to allow pilots of conventional tricycle undercarriage aircraft to fly in without doing some careful sums first. The maths involved is simply checking from the aircraft *Owner's Manual* or *Pilot's Operating Handbook* the exact landing and take-off distances required by the aircraft at the weight involved, and correlating this with the actual air temperature and wind velocity. The handbook figure must then be factored appropriately using the data provided by the CAA in their AIC on take-off, landing and climb performance of light aeroplanes (currently AIC 12/1996, though this gets regularly updated). Grass surfaces can require greatly extended take-off and landing distances as compared with concrete or asphalt surfaces. The difference can be as much as 30% if the grass is wet and less than 8 inches high, and up to 60% for landings on short, wet, slippery grass, to give just a couple of examples. Some strips have been laid on appreciably sloping ground; this significantly affects performance figures and you must also take this into consideration. If you are at all doubtful about your ability to get in to the chosen strip and out again in safety, forget it. There are lots more places to land and no strip owner welcomes bent aeroplanes cluttering up his little airfield. They (and their neighbours) don't welcome noisy visitors either, so for their sake (and for the future existence of the strip too, in case it is under threat from local protesters) please fly especially quietly and considerately in its vicinity. Keep to the approved circuit procedure, avoid flying directly over noise sensitive places (which you should enquire about if they don't tell you when you ring for prior permission) and avoid dragging your aircraft in on a noisy, long-drawn-out low approach under power. And once you have rolled to a stop don't forget that Rule 17(7) of Rules of the Air requires you to turn first to the left after landing, even if you *know* you are the only aircraft for miles around and the parking area happens to be to the right. The law just happens to be the law, and there just *might* be someone else flying in, about whom you were blissfully unaware.

Making use of little fields like these gives a whole new feel to your flying. Dropping in (after getting the essential prior permission) to a peaceful grass strip to meet like-minded friends, to have a picnic perhaps, or to overnight in a convenient pub nearby, is a totally different experience to flying in to even a small licensed aerodrome. The informality appeals greatly to many pilots, even if the more hide-bound big-fielders amongst us may find it unappealing. Care must be taken though, to ensure that not too much of the informality creeps into the actual flying. Grass strips demand a higher degree of precision flying than most bigger airfields. They can, and not infrequently do, punish pilots who have the temerity to treat them with too casual an attitude.

Other Countries; Other Customs

As has been said several times already, a great deal of enjoyment can be had from flying in foreign lands. British-based pilots have first to overcome any innate reluctance they may have about flying over water in order to experience the joys of flying in the rest of Europe in their own, or their rented G-registered aeroplane. If you are not convinced of the fact that aircraft engines have no means of telling whether they are over land or water and run just as reliably on air with a traditional whiff of seaside ozone in it as they do anywhere else, then pick a short sea crossing. From England to the nearest landfall in continental Europe is a mere 19 nm and, with no controlled airspace under FL65 between Dover and Calais, you can fly VFR, weather permitting, at say 4,500 or 5,500 feet. From 5,500 feet a typical four-seat single, of average performance, has a still air gliding range of around nine nautical miles with the propeller windmilling. Thus, on the short passage across the Strait of Dover, there is but a very brief interval of time when you couldn't suffer a total power loss and still be able to glide back to land without even getting your feet wet. Similarly, only 22 nm of salt water separates southern Scotland from Northern Ireland and so even those pilots who remain slightly nervous about overwater flight should be able to reach Ireland without too much anxiety.

Pilots of light singles frequently tackle quite lengthy stretches of water, quietly confident that their aero-engine will keep on turning in exactly the same way it has always done over land. Flying from Scotland via the Strait of Dover for a visit to Scandinavia is rather a long way round and the 270 nm Aberdeen to Stavanger route is used by quite a few VFR pilots every year. It means a fraction over two hours out of sight of land in an average light aircraft, but with appropriate survival equipment on board this seems to worry some pilots very little. Compared with the way singles are regularly ferried across the Atlantic via Greenland and Iceland it is indeed a mere nothing in terms of water crossings.

Renting Abroad

Not all private pilots have enough of the Lindbergh spirit though, and there is an alternative way of flying abroad which might appeal more to them. This involves taking ferries or scheduled airlines to the chosen area and then renting a suitable aircraft there. Within Europe at the time of writing there are still some complications concerning validation of UK PPLs to allow you to use them when flying as pilot in command of certain foreign registered aircraft. This situation is changing though, and I fully expect that shortly all that will be required to pilot a light aircraft in any of the JAA countries will be a European licence issued under the JAR/FCL regulations. That, together with a check-out that will almost certainly be asked for by whoever is renting the aeroplane out. Outside Europe the situation varies. In the United States the FAA will issue an Airman's Certificate quickly and easily on the evidence of your own national licence. Elsewhere regulations vary from what is little more than a cursory glance at your logbook and licence, to what amounts to almost going through another PPL written examination and GFT. It can often be well worth the effort though. I have lasting and wonderful memories of the flying I was able to do following a morning spent studying New Zealand's VFR regulations and then passing an examination about them in a stuffy office in Auckland. It opened the door to an aviator's paradise of islands, miles of sandy beaches, volcanoes, hot springs, glaciers, fjords and some of the friendliest flying clubs and most fascinating flyers in the world. And having all the local rules and regulations fresh in my mind also helped me to relax and enjoy these wonderful holiday flying experiences.

VFR Variations

When in foreign lands, don't assume that what is standard practice at home will also be accepted as such there. Even the definition of what is VFR varies from country to country. In some countries, currently including France, Belgium, Norway, the Republic of Ireland, Italy and Germany 'VFR on top' (ie flying above a closed layer of cloud, out of sight of the surface) is permitted (provided you can get up there and back down again without going IMC). Elsewhere it is illegal. Some pilots seem to believe that an imaginary hole in the cloud layer below them somewhere near their destination is sufficient to enable them to comply with 'VFR on Top' regulations where this is permitted. Possibly it may be, provided their navigation is perfect (or their GPS doesn't lead them astray) but they should try not to forget the famous words of Antoine de St Exupéry *'If a pilot is wrong ... just below the sea of clouds begins eternity'*.

The limitations defining Special VFR vary considerably from one European country to another and sometimes (as in France) between one aerodrome control zone and another within the same country. Many countries either totally forbid VFR flying between sunset and sunrise or so severely restrict it as to make it virtually impossible. Elsewhere it is perfectly legal; in the UK all night VFR within a CTR has to be Special VFR, whilst outside controlled airspace all PPL holders who have a night, rating may fly at night, provided they observe normal VFR weather minima, quadrantal cruising levels and minimum height rules. Such flights are conducted under IFR but can be executed virtually as if they were VFR flights.

The IMC rating does not exist outside the UK and holders of an IMC rating are prohibited from using any of its privileges outside UK airspace. Also the UK's quadrantal height rule is used only in a few countries of the former British Empire which have retained it. In its place you should familiarise yourself with the semicircular rule used in most other states. This specifies that, above 3,000 ft for tracks from 000° M to 179° M you should fly at FL35, FL55, FL75, FL95 etc up to FL195 while for tracks from 180° M to 359° M you should fly at FL45, FL65, FL85 etc up to FL185.

Skulking along keeping below the base of the airways system is part and parcel of normal VFR in the airspace of the UK, but in much of the rest of the world either airways virtually don't exist below FL100 (as in Germany and the USA) or VFR traffic is permitted to fly within the airways system, at least up to a specified flight level (as in the Republic of Ireland, France, Belgium, Spain, Portugal, Denmark, Greece, Switzerland etc). In the Netherlands, VFR traffic is banned from airways, in much the same way as in the UK.

The system used when you are approaching aerodromes with control towers, follows much the same routine the world over, but there are some European countries (eg Switzerland) where the use of VFR reporting points (VRPs) is mandatory. This makes it essential for you to have with you appropriate landing charts from a flight guide or from the AIP. Even if these are not necessities in other countries I would certainly recommend you to have them with you anywhere you go. They make life simpler both for you and for the controllers. When you are heading for a small airfield in a country other than the one you normally fly in, and you are expecting to have to make a conventional circuit join, don't assume that the conventions here will necessarily be the same as they are at home. They probably won't be. Circuit heights can vary from as little as 500 ft above aerodrome level to 1,200 ft or more. In Germany the joining procedure is similar to the UK, but in France locals expect you to descend over the aerodrome to join downwind from the inside at about its mid-point. In the USA you are expected to join downwind from an angle of about 45°, again about midway along it, but this time from the outside of the circuit. (And the word 'circuit' is pretty meaningless in the USA; call it the 'pattern' and they'll understand you better.) In the Netherlands a standard join is similar to the American one, except that you are expected to approach the downwind leg at 90 to it, not 45, and then turn right or left depending on the circuit direction. Belgian pilots are generally taught to join downwind right at its start, by coming towards it from a long way upwind; this system has the advantage of letting pilots size up the traffic situation pretty thoroughly. As a visitor in a foreign land you are expected to conform to local circuit procedures, so a little investigation of this subject in advance is highly advisable.

Minimum height rules are another area where unsuspecting visiting pilots might find themselves under misconceptions. The UK's 'closer than 500 feet to any person, vessel, vehicle or structure' (which makes low flying across open moorland legal, provided you avoid any hikers or houses by at least 500 ft horizontally, diagonally or vertically) doesn't necessarily apply elsewhere. The French have a complex table of minimum heights relating to what you are overflying and what type of aircraft you are in. For piston singles 1,000 ft is required from factories, hospitals and motorways, 1,500 ft from small gatherings, towns and herds of cattle and so on up to 4,500 ft for big built-up areas and gatherings of over 100,000 persons. The AIPs of certain countries actually specify that it is forbidden to fly underneath bridges or similar constructions but even when this veto has not actually been put into print it is still probably wisest to assume it exists!

The process of adapting to local conventions whilst flying abroad is greatly eased by getting hold of a copy of the local AIP and spending a couple of hours studying it before venturing into the air. For France the *Delage Guide* makes a good starting point (if you understand enough French) and the French AIS publish an indispensable set of four 1:1,000,000 VFR charts, a 1:250,000 chart of the Paris area and a VFR Guide. This set is updated every April and November, so make sure you have the current set before you fly. Many other countries (eg Germany, Belgium, the Netherlands) publish special official VFR Guides to assist VFR pilots visiting their lands. *Bottlang Airfield Manuals* and *Pooley's European Flight Guides* all contain some useful basic information about local procedures but most countries keep the occasional surprise to spring on their visiting pilots. There are things like Germany's flashing yellow lights at the end of the runway; these are not simple navigation aids, they are illuminated to prohibit take-off or landing of powered aircraft during glider operations. In France the frequency 123.50MHz is the AeroClub 'common', much used for local chat and many French pilots are dreadfully disappointed to find it doesn't work outside their own skies. Over Greece it is illegal to take photographs using telephoto lenses. In Norway there are large wild reindeer areas where flight below 1,000 ft is forbidden, but the Norwegians do sell a useful money saving season ticket that can pay for all the landing charges that a foreign-registered aircraft under 2 tonnes incurs for seven consecutive days. The Spanish take PPR specially seriously; if an aerodrome is listed as PPR in the official *Aerodrome Directory* then you must have prior permission before you may even put it on a flight plan as an alternate, never mind actually land there. There are three so-called 'N-areas' in Sweden and it is forbidden to fly in any of these unless a flight plan has been submitted either 20 minutes before take-off within the area, or 20 minutes prior to flying into it. Do any VFR flying in the United States and you will soon encounter their infamous Unicom system of RT communication. This is an aeronautical advisory service in which several airfields all share the same VHF frequency, so you are liable to hear a cacophony of pilots' voices all calling traffic advisories for different places. Since Unicom should only be used while you are close to the airfield in question, and since all calls are prefaced with the airfield name, what looks like a recipe for RT chaos actually works out reasonably well, as is proved by the fact that Unicom has been used successfully for many years all over the States.

Unusual UK

If you do most of your flying in UK airspace you may well be beginning to think by now that it would be so much better if other countries could arrange their VFR as simply and sensibly as we do here. Think again. Pilots visiting our skies have to get accustomed to such peculiarities as Purple Airways, which don't appear on any ICAO charts; two sets of SVFR minima, one for PPL holders and one for PPL holders with a mysterious thing called an IMC Rating; a total ban on flying in all that virtually empty airspace that forms the lower levels of UK airways; LARS, which they will never have met under that title anywhere else; and that famous and almost unique quadrantal rule already referred to.

One day perhaps the JAA will manage to harmonize VFR throughout Europe. The FAA doesn't tolerate differences like these between California and Florida, or Texas and Idaho. This undoubtedly does make flying under VFR around the USA a great deal simpler than flying VFR around Europe. Variety is said to be the spice of life, however, and there is no doubt that these varied European interpretations of the basic ICAO Visual Flight Rules, all help to add quite a lot to the spice of flying under VFR as a private pilot around this continent.

Chapter 5

Cash and Carry

Financing Your Flying

Throughout your flying training the cash flow was all in one direction, out of your own pocket into the coffers of the flying club or school that was providing your training. With your new PPL tucked safely in your probably somewhat empty pocket, your mind may well soon turn to thoughts about just what you can do to ease the financial burden that is involved in making use of your licence.

If the establishment where you trained is one of those where most of the time they require all their fleet of aircraft for flying training work, they may well have decided to set a fairly expensive price for you to hire these machines for solo flying or touring. Because of this, you obviously want to look around for a somewhat less expensive place from which to rent your aircraft. The hourly rates for solo flying do vary surprisingly, even for similar aircraft with similar levels of avionics and other equipment. A check through the 'Where to Fly' pages that appeared in 1996 in *Pilot* and *Flyer* magazines for instance, showed that the hourly rate for solo flight in a Cessna 152 can be as little as £56 in one place and as much as £75 in another. Four-seat aircraft rates likewise are far from standard throughout the country; C172, Piper Archer or Grumman Cheetah aircraft can be hired for about £65 per hour from some clubs, whilst elsewhere pilots can be asked for well over £100 per hour for similar machines. Okay, the level of radio and other equipment in the different aircraft will certainly vary a bit from one to another. Other things, such as whether an expensive club membership is involved and whether local landing charges are, or are not, included in the quoted hourly rate, are also significant factors. You should be sure to find out about and consider these items when you are weighing up the various rates on offer. None the less, even a simple comparison like this shows that a little shopping around the local area can often be quite a help in reducing the negative flow of your hard-earned cash each time you rent an aircraft to fly.

There is, of course, one very big question to answer in connection with your future flying. Should you really go on renting aircraft to fly at all? It might be a much better plan for you, depending on all the relevant circumstances, either to buy a share in an aircraft or to become an aircraft owner yourself. These options are dealt with in more detail in Chapter 8. There are many other ways of cutting the costs of continuing to fly, although not always in conventional light aircraft. These can include moving to microlights, taking up parachuting, becoming a sailplane enthusiast or jumping off mountains as a hang-glider pilot. We take a look at the first of these (microlighting) also in Chapter 8, together with the idea of building your own aircraft. Parachuting and gliding in all their various forms are, however, beyond the scope of this book, which is intended essentially to show private pilots how much enjoyment they can derive from making full use of their licences, and PPLs do not really have all that much bearing on these other airborne activities.

PPL–No Licence to Print Money

Enjoyment you can certainly get from using a Private Pilot's Licence; income you cannot. A Private Pilot's Licence entitles the holder under the Air Navigation Order to fly as pilot in command, or co-pilot, of any aeroplane within the aircraft rating included in the licence, subject to the very important exclusion of *'flying any such aeroplane for the purposes of public transport or aerial work'*. You can carry out aerial work only in a few strictly limited ways. If you have an instructor's or assistant flying instructor's rating you are entitled to give flying instruction and to carry out flying tests provided you, the student and the aircraft, are all part and parcel of the same flying club. Similarly, if you are a member of a gliding or a parachuting club, you can undertake aerial work so long as this is limited to towing a glider or flying an aircraft used for dropping parachutists, again provided the aircraft is owned or operated by, and all the people concerned are members of, the club involved. Even then though, no PPL holder is entitled to receive any remuneration for flying the aircraft. The sole exception to that rule is when the aeroplane is a microlight or a self-launching motor glider and it is being used for instruction or testing on that type of aircraft, and provided that you have an appropriate instructor's rating. In that case you may receive remuneration for the instruction given or the testing conducted. Otherwise, as a private pilot you are prohibited from receiving any remuneration whatsoever for any of the flying you do.

Another legal requirement makes the matter of financing your PPL flying even more problematic. This is the requirement that any operator of a UK registered aircraft who utilises the aircraft for public transport must hold an Air Operator's Certificate (AOC) issued by the CAA. This applies even if the aircraft is to be used in this way for only one single flight. The definition of a 'public transport flight' is very simple and straightforward; it is 'any flight which carries passengers and/or cargo for valuable consideration'. And 'valuable consideration' can be taken to mean simply, if the owner or operator gains financially or otherwise from the fact that the flight took place. The CAA has prosecuted a number of uncertificated operators who have transgressed this all-embracing law. Both the pilots and the operators also run the other risk that their insurance company might well wriggle out of its liability in respect of any policy if an aircraft were to be used for public transport without an AOC being held.

Sharing Expenses

It is, however, legal for the holder of a Private Pilot's Licence to share the expenses of certain types of flight without the operator being required to hold an AOC. The pilot must bear a proportional share of the actual costs of the flight. This means half the total costs if there are two on board, one third if three people fly together and one quarter if there are four in the aircraft. No more than four persons, including any children, may be on board. The flight must not have been advertised, except that when it is a club aircraft it may be advertised within the club and all on board must be members of that club and over eighteen years of age. The pilot must not be under contract to, or employed by, the operator of the aircraft. Abide by these rules and, although you obviously cannot make a profit, you can (at least so long as you can find suitable co-pilots or passengers to accompany you) reduce the effective cost of your flying.

If your employer is prepared to reimburse you the actual costs of a flight made for business purposes then, provided you were not actually *obliged* by your employer to make that flight, you can, as a private pilot, legally reclaim these costs. You break the rules if you try to make a profit from the flight, but you can recover all the actual costs involved. This is relatively easy to do if you are renting or hiring the aircraft being used. You can reclaim the actual hire cost as invoiced to you, plus any landing charges, parking or hangar fees incurred, and fuel and oil bills. But the situation is less clear-cut for the owner pilot. Claiming back from your employer a sum equivalent to the cost of alternative transport might be perfectly okay from your boss's point of view, but might not satisfy the CAA. A business class air fare, or the price of a first class rail ticket might be considered to represent more than the actual costs incurred in using the aircraft, thus giving you as pilot a financial benefit on the deal. Even if you were to use the equivalent cost of travel for the same journey in your own car (using the so-called Fixed Profit Car Scheme (FPCS) mileage cost figures as approved by the taxman) this might still cause CAA eyebrows to be raised, even if your tax inspector would almost certainly accept the figures. To claim back the equivalent of what the hire would have been for a similar aircraft from a nearby club should be acceptable, but even then lawyers could argue that this must include a certain element of profit. The only legally watertight procedure for the owner-pilot would be to reclaim purely and simply the direct costs of the flight (fuel, oil, landings, hangarage etc) and to swallow hard and ignore such things as depreciation, insurance, maintenance etc since it can always be argued that these would still have to be borne, whether or not that specific business flight had been undertaken.

Exceptions to the Rule

If you are into competition flying, you as a private pilot can, within limits, actually earn something from air racing. You are permitted whilst flying with a PPL to collect prize money (or remuneration in the form of fuel/expenses) up to a value of £500 per event. Whether this would ever cover your actual costs of practice, entry and competing in the event is another matter entirely. And after all, you did it for the honour and glory, the fun, thrills and excitement and not for the money anyway, didn't you?

Provided you obtain permission from the CAA for a flight in aid of a registered charity (in advance of the flight) you are also allowed to collect payment for the flight, on condition that this payment (and that means all of it without any deduction for expenses or anything else) is applied for the benefit of the charity. Again, I have to admit that this doesn't do anything at all for you in the way of helping you to finance your flying, but at least it is one way of getting some hours into your log book that should make you feel good too, at least for a while.

There is only one other set of circumstances in which money can legally be paid to a PPL in connection with the cost of flying, and that is detailed in Chapter 8 where the question of group ownership of an aircraft is being considered.

In addition to the few legally permitted forms of remuneration described above, you will probably hear about lots of other wheezes whereby club bores and hangar-pilots claim they have managed to cover the costs of at least some of their flying. Some are downright contraventions of the law. You hear about such exploits as the chap who flew a couple of blokes who were in a tearing hurry to get to the Isle of Man and who 'covered the cost of the petrol' with a wad of well-thumbed twenty-pound notes. This is blatantly illegal, brazenly immoral, probably uninsured and is certainly depriving air taxi operators and CPL qualified pilots of their bread and butter. In the same way, any PPL qualified pilot who accepts any form of remuneration for the transportation of goods, whether these goods be no more than an urgent letter or as much as a cabin full of freight, is acting illegally, and risking prosecution and the loss of his or her licence. This sort of behaviour is simply not acceptable.

Some indirect forms of remuneration seem to fall into a grey area, despite their not appearing to be authorised by the Air Navigation Order. Take the private pilot who goes off to some romantic place on holiday and writes up his or her exploits for *Popular Flying*, *Pilot*, *Flyer* or possibly (if it was that sort of holiday) for *Cosmopolitan* or *Penthouse*. If our hypothetical literary pilot is lucky, or is a particularly good writer, the cheque in payment for the article might possibly more than cover the cost of the flying involved. Could that be construed as receiving remuneration for the flying? Or would it always be accepted that the flying was only incidental and that any such income was payment purely and simply for the writing? If a PPL holder undertakes flights with the specific objective of photographing stately (or not so stately) homes, hotels or factories etc and then proceeds to sell these photographs to defray the cost of the flying, this amounts to illegally undertaking aerial work. That is quite definitely excluded from the privileges of the PPL. But on the other hand, the circumstances could be that in the course of a pleasure flight a private pilot took some photographs, then later decided to enter some in a competition and one of these happened to win a nice cash prize. Or possibly some of them might later be sold, maybe quite a long time after the flight on which they were taken, as illustrations for a book. In such a case it would appear to me (and here I must emphasise that I am not a lawyer) that it would be difficult to prove that any income of this nature had arisen from the pilot having carried out some aerial work illegally without a commercial licence and the necessary AOC.

If in Doubt, Ask an Expert

One must remember, however, the old adage about the law being an ass and this can at times tend to leave the poor private pilot wondering where exactly the line should be drawn between inadvertent infringement of the law and innocent enjoyment of the hobby of flying. If you end up confronted by any situation of this nature, best get hold of an authoritative book dealing with aviation law and study it carefully. Then remember that if you are still in doubt about some aspect of whatever is afoot, you ought always to err on the safe side. Tax experts often give their clients the advice that bending the tax rules and statutes is one thing but breaking them is quite another. In the case of PPL pilots and aerial work the situation is similar; be careful that you do not cross the line, indistinct as that line sometimes may appear to be.

There are many other instances, as I am sure the reader can imagine, where some form of income could arise either directly or indirectly from private piloting. If you are ever tempted to tackle anything of a dubious nature my advice to you is to avoid it like the plague. If it is anything that looks to you as though it might require an AOC, don't touch it, even with the proverbial barge pole. If anyone tries to inveigle you into doing any form of paid flying that falls more properly within the province of a CPL or ATPL qualified pilot, it is wiser not to take the risk. If you yield to the temptation to do anything of that nature you are much more likely to put your licence into serious jeopardy than to help cover some of the costs of your flying.

Tax Breaks

There are certain ways in which some pilots can reduce the effective cost of their flying by making use of tax concessions and relief on Income Tax, Corporation Tax and VAT. There isn't much scope here for you if you are taxed conventionally through the PAYE system, but if you are fortunate enough to be running a business of your own you could possibly benefit. In order to do so, it is necessary to justify any claim for tax relief associated with an aeroplane in terms of the relevant Income Tax and Corporation Tax Acts and their current interpretation. You have to take care here too. The said interpretation (and the Acts themselves) are constantly changing as Chancellors, courts and appeal bodies go about their work. This is a positive minefield for the unwary and I strongly suggest that any reader thinking about trying to claim tax relief in connection with flying light aeroplanes go straight off to consult a professional tax adviser. I am not an expert in that field and these paragraphs are not in any way intended as a guide to gaining tax relief for a private aeroplane. Unless you can convince yourself that your aircraft has really been, or will be, of use to your business, don't bother trying to convince the tax authorities. Only legitimate claims have any real chance of success.

There are two different sets of people involved here. One of these bodies is the Inland Revenue, who deal with Income and Corporation Tax and the other is Customs and Excise, who administer Value Added Tax. Their approach to the question of the use of an aircraft within a business may not necessarily be the same. To claim back the VAT on the purchase of an aircraft it is necessary to justify to the VAT Office that the aircraft is a business asset, similar, tax-wise, to an office desk, word processor, delivery truck or warehouse. This usually requires proof that it is actually used either as business transport or for advertising purposes. If you claim it is business transport, be careful; you could then fall foul of the requirement that you must have a Commercial Pilot's Licence before you can legally do aerial work. If you claim it is used for advertising, the advertising logos on the aircraft must be prominent enough to be seen and your business such that this type of advertising might reasonably be expected to attract new customers to it. If the Tax Inspector can be convinced that the aircraft really is playing an important role in your business, then you may be able to claim capital allowances, which have the effect of spreading the cost of the aircraft as tax relief over a number of years. There are certain further advantages in having the aircraft accepted as being part of the business. Many of the operating costs, such as fuel, maintenance, hangarage and insurance can become business expenses and, assuming your business is VAT registered, the VAT can also be reclaimed on most of these items. Finally, if your personal tax position should ever come under close scrutiny, it could be very useful to have all your aircraft costs already neatly accounted for in the business books, rather than have a cynical Tax Inspector querying how you can possibly afford to run an expensive plaything like an aircraft on the meagre taxable income that you are declaring!

The matter of borrowing money to finance the purchase of an aircraft is dealt with later in this chapter, but there is at least one other type of loan that could interest some private pilots. This is an advance to help pay for flying training towards advanced ratings and qualifications. If your ultimate intention is to make a career as a commercial pilot there are several UK banks which currently operate loan schemes which they make available to embryo CPL pilots for this purpose. Courses leading to NVQ or SVQ also carry tax break possibilities. These systems and regulations do tend to change fairly frequently and for that reason (plus the fact that this book is not really designed for the private pilot who is heading for a CPL) these are not listed in detail here.

Risky Up-Front Payments

If you are wealthy enough to pay in advance the whole (or a substantial amount) of the fee for any particular flying training course, it is often possible to obtain what sounds like quite an interesting discount on the basic price. If you are dealing with a well-established school or club this is quite frequently a very sensible way for you to cut down on the cost of the advanced training. However, pilots should always be on their guard. In rather too many cases where this discount is heavily promoted by the establishment concerned, it has proved to be a symptom of the fact that the school was in a somewhat unsatisfactory financial state. It probably was, in fact, in dire need of the advance payment in its coffers to keep itself financially afloat. If, as sometimes happened, the school sank before the pilot's course had been completed, he or she was left high and dry with no qualification, no cash, and often precious little chance of recouping much of the advance deposit as an ordinary creditor of the bankrupt establishment. There have even been a few cases of deliberately fraudulent operations being set up simply to collect as much as possible in the way of cash advances from unsuspecting pilots, before the perpetrators vanish into the night, complete with all the gullible pilots' cash. Check the credentials of any establishment carefully before you decide to part with any flying training fees up front like this.

Obtaining a Loan

If on the other hand you are less affluent, you may need to obtain a loan towards the not insignificant costs of training for an IMC rating, multi-engine rating or PPL/IR (see Chapter 6). There are several potential sources of cash available for these purposes, although I am not aware of any schemes designed specifically for private pilots who want to train for advanced qualifications. Many high street banks seem to be put off lending for anything that is in any way connected with private flying, but some bank managers do seem to be more relaxed about this and are quite prepared to consider a loan for advanced flying training. This normally only happens for pilots whom they already know as existing customers of the bank and who are considered by them to be suitable borrowers. Banks will usually make the proviso that the loan is secured on a life insurance policy or on your home . . . always assuming that your home is not already mortgaged up to the hilt. If your own bank manager cannot or will not come up with what you require, there are other sources of outside finance worth looking at. Many financial institutions are prepared to grant secured loans, normally using property or life insurance policies as the necessary security, but pilots applying for one of these loans as new customers can expect to pay quite a bit over the odds in interest. Likewise, loans can be had, based on your own personal credit rating, from other finance companies and credit brokers. Several of these have departments specialising in aviation loans and will generally be quite happy to advance cash to be used for flying qualifications, aircraft purchase, engine replacement etc to pilots whom they consider creditworthy clients. The classified advertisements at the back of *Pilot* and *Flyer* magazines are good places to look for phone numbers and addresses for such companies. Also Pilot members of AOPA UK will find that this organisation has links with one or two finance companies who would be prepared to consider making money available to them for these purposes. Be sure you are aware of all aspects of what you are taking on before you sign on any dotted lines though. As the advertisements say, your home may be at risk if you fail to keep up the repayments on any mortgage or other loan that is secured on it. Also, many loans of this nature are significantly more expensive in interest terms than a straight overdraft would be if you could persuade your bank to give you the cash for your advanced flying qualification in that form instead.

To the outsider, private flying has always carried with it an aura of enormous expense. It is generally considered to be a sport or pastime available only to the very affluent. However, to most enthusiasts, private flying is an activity for which sacrifices have to be willingly made. If it all gets to be too much of a strain (either on the finances or on the spare time) to keep other activities like golf or skiing going, then these just get demoted in the keen pilot's order of priorities. If the family car is still running well, then it is always better to carry on running it for another year or two, rather than buy a new model, if that would eat too far into your flying budget. If a half-hour in the club's nice shiny 180 hp four-seat tourer swallows up too much of your monthly pay cheque, then a couple of circuits in the clapped-out old two-seat trainer is far better then no flying at all. If you find enough fun and fascination in your flying, you'll always manage to find enough finance to keep flying somehow.

Loans to Buy Aircraft

In Chapter 8 we take a look at the pros and cons of aircraft ownership and (just in case you find more pros than cons in your own case) this chapter would not be complete without some consideration of how to go about financing the purchase of an aeroplane of your own.

By far the most economical way is always to buy the aircraft out of capital if that is an available option in your own circumstances. The loss of interest on a savings account is invariably a great deal less than the interest you will have to pay on any form of loan you take out for this purpose. Unfortunately not all PPLs with an urge to become aircraft owners are in the fortunate position of having the necessary amount of cash available or easily realisable.

As mentioned above in connection with bank loans for flying training, not all bank managers have a very high opinion of light aviation. Although they are usually quite happy to lend money for their customers to purchase Peugeots or Porches, they take a very different attitude towards a customer whose mind runs in the direction of Bonanzas or Beagles. A personal loan from a bank which knows you is usually the next best thing to an overdraft for this purpose, but if this is not available, once again a good place to look for details of other lenders who have a more sympathetic attitude towards aeroplanes is in the back pages of *Pilot* and *Flyer* among the classified ads. AOPA UK also claims to have negotiated special rates for their members with certain loan companies. Once again however, the same caveat as before; this type of finance is not the cheapest around, so it is important to check very carefully what you are letting yourself in for before you enter into any binding contract to borrow in this way to help you to buy your aeroplane. You can very easily end up repaying vastly more than the basic cost of the aircraft, especially if the loan is taken out over a number of years. Even a reputable credit broker who advances you a loan of £25,000, which is to be paid back over a period of ten years, is likely to be demanding monthly repayments which will add up to a figure that is closer to £50,000 than £25,000 by the end of the ten years. Best take an electronic calculator with you while you do your negotiations, and be on your guard!

Pilots who buy their aircraft from a reputable second-hand aircraft dealer, or are lucky enough to be buying a new machine direct from the manufacturer or the official distributor, will certainly find it well worth enquiring whether they have a financing scheme available. If they have made special arrangements with a finance company this can often turn out to be an appreciably less expensive route to a loan for you as purchaser, than any direct approach you might make to an outside finance company. Since the seller usually will also earn some commission from the loan contract you enter into (in the same way as in the case of car dealers) it is also worth trying to use this fact to lever a keener price for the aircraft. If your purchase is being made directly from another private aircraft owner you will almost certainly have to arrange any necessary finance yourself. Just make sure you allow yourself sufficient time to arrange the least expensive type of loan that is available. Don't be too impetuous and end up saddling yourself with unnecessary extra expenses. Believe me, you will enjoy your new acquisition much more if you have enough cash left over, after paying off the money-lenders, to fly the aeroplane from time to time and maybe eat occasionally too.

Chapter 6

Breaking New Ground

Night Flight

Perhaps it is because most private pilots earn their licences without ever flying in the dark that it never occurs to many of them to obtain a night rating. After all, they reason, they've no intention of ever flying at night, so what's the point? Isn't night flying dangerous, especially in single-engine aircraft, and aren't night ratings difficult and expensive to obtain? Better really, when all's said and done, just to leave flying in the dark to the professionals. Not many birds fly after sunset, so why the hell should I?

But none of that is necessarily true. A night rating is one of the easiest and least expensive ratings you can 'add on' to a PPL. Learning the basics of night flying extends your experience of airmanship in general and will help make you a better pilot. Flying in the dark is not inherently all that more risky than flying in daylight, given that the pilot in command is competent and is willing to take a few sensible precautions. Even for pilots who have no intention of flying after sunset, a night rating can be a very useful insurance against the day when they are delayed, perhaps by weather or by passengers or air traffic control, and inadvertently find darkness creeping up on them before they can reach their destination.

Night flight can provide you with a marvellously enjoyable, almost ethereal experience, totally different from daylight piloting. It opens up new facets of airmanship, new sights and new satisfactions, as well as helping to eliminate that feeling of impending crisis if you are ever confronted in the air by a fast approaching sunset. This is altogether too good a thing to leave just to the professionals. Amateur pilots are perfectly capable of tackling darkness professionally too.

With the exception of flight under the supervision of a qualified flying instructor, no PPL pilot may fly at night unless he or she has a night rating. To carry passengers at night as a PPL holder you must have a night rating and must also have carried out, as pilot in command, within the preceding thirteen months, not less than five night take-offs and five night landings. Strangely enough, to qualify as a 'night' take-off or landing it is not sufficient that it takes place between 30 minutes after sunset and 30 minutes before sunrise (which is the definition of official 'night' for logbook entry purposes). The depression of the centre of the sun must, according to the Air Navigation Order, be not less than 12° below the horizon for your take-offs and landings to qualify for validation of your night rating. They don't always count, just because you do them while it's dark! And conversely, they do count even if you do them when there is a brilliant full moon making the night almost as bright as day.

As soon as you have 50 hours logged (of which at least 25 are as pilot in command) you can head for your night rating. Experience requirements include at least five hours instruction in instrument flying and five hours night flying under the supervision of a QFI. Usefully, all this flying can also count towards the requirements for what might turn out to be your next step, the IMC or the instrument rating (IR). Once you qualify for your night rating too, there is no need to undergo regular re-testing to renew it. You are then entitled to fly at night, solo or whilst carrying passengers, any time you please so long as you have logged five night take-offs and five night landings within the preceding 13 months. If you allow yourself to go beyond the 13 month period without carrying out sufficient take-offs and landings to keep the rating valid, you have only to make the required number of take-offs and landings to bring the total up to five within 13 months to revalidate your rating. You can do this either with, or under the supervision of, a flying instructor but it is illegal to take anyone with you during these flights, other than the instructor. Thereafter you are free to carry passengers at night again.

Within the UK, Channel Islands and Isle of Man airspace, no VFR flight is permitted at night (ie from 30 minutes after sunset until 30 minutes before sunrise and so for flights at night, pilots must fly IFR. This does *not* mean that an instrument rating is necessary to fly at night, only that flight outside controlled airspace must be conducted within the limitations of the pilot's licence, which must be at least a PPL with a valid night rating. The pilot must also comply with the minimum height rule (1000ft above the highest obstacle within 5nm of track) and, if operating above 3000ft amsl, must fly in accordance with the quadrantal rule. VFR is not permitted within Class A airspace at any time, and if the night flight involves flying within a Control Zone that peculiar form of IFR clearance known as a Special VFR clearance must be requested from ATC.

It can be Different in the Dark

Don't assume that as the holder of a UK night rating you can automatically fly at night under similar regulations in all other countries. Despite the European harmonisation of regulations under JAR mentioned in Chapter 4, wide variations still exist in VFR night flying rules. Night VFR is not permitted at all in, for example, the Netherlands, Spain, Italy and Denmark. Special permission must be obtained to fly night VFR in Austria, Greece, Iceland and the Republic of Ireland. It is restricted to varying extents in Belgium, Luxembourg, France and Finland. Within Europe, it is only in the UK, Germany, Switzerland, Norway and Sweden, where you can be fairly certain of being able to exercise the privileges of your night rating without too many restrictions. In fact in several of these countries you can fly VFR at night as well as during daylight hours. In the United States the FAA has not thought it necessary to ban the world's largest GA population from night VFR.

Presumably the reason the authorities in so many countries do ban, or severely restrict, night VFR is that they regard it as being inherently dangerous. But it is, in point of fact, no exotic adventure, no rash, uncalculated risk. There is, admittedly, always some risk of inadvertently flying into IMC in the dark. Clouds are much more difficult to spot at night than during the day but if at night the ground lights and stars all unexpectedly fade from sight, it is probably high time you executed that 180° safety turn to regain visual conditions. A thorough study of the forecast weather before night flying is always a must. The other big worry is of course engine failure, especially in a single-engine aircraft. Aero-engines are, on the whole, remarkably reliable beasts, but if the donkey ever did decide to die on you at night in a single, you would be the first to admit that it all suddenly becomes a great deal more stressful than in broad daylight. One fatalistic piece of 'advice' for such an occasion is to aim for a dark piece of terrain (so you would most probably be heading for open country or woodland and keeping clear of the collision hazard of buildings), then switch on your landing light when you reckon you are about a couple of hundred feet above the ground and, if you don't like what you see, just switch the light off again quickly and start praying.

Electrical failure too can put more additional pressure on you if it occurs at night than it is ever likely to do in daylight. Which is one more good reason for carrying not just the obligatory torch for map and instrument reading, but also spare batteries and a bulb . . . or even better a complete spare torch. (It is much easier swapping torches than trying to swap a fiddly little bulb whilst flying an aeroplane in total darkness!)

Nocturnal Niceties

Flying at night can be a delightful experience. There are fewer aircraft in the air and those that are flying are easier to see with their colourful strobes, flashing beacons and navigation lights twinkling. The radio has less chatter on it and is sometimes a little less formal. The night air is frequently far smoother than by day, devoid of thermal turbulence. The aircraft often seems to slip silkily through the sky in a way you seldom otherwise enjoy. The view of an urban landscape at night can be unexpectedly beautiful, in contrast to its normally drab daytime appearance. Skeins of lights, mercury blue, tungsten white and sodium yellow, trace the lines of roads and streets with ribbons of vehicle headlights trickling past them. Shop lights, factory signs, floodlit sports grounds, advertisements and traffic lights all help transform even an ugly industrial landscape into something resembling fairyland. Even a couple of thousand feet above the surface at night you are often clear of much of the dust and smoke that dulls the natural sparkle of the stars. Flight on a cloudless night can then provide an unforgettable spectacle of the starry heavens, each pinpoint of light shining with a clarity you seldom can see from ground level. A moonlit night too can provide a memorable flight; black hills etched against the luminescent sky, silvery lakes against the dark background of open country and maybe breaking waves sparkling in the lunar light along a coastline. Night flying is for lovers, for poets and all romantics.

Numerous books are available on the subject of night flying, covering the techniques of navigation at night, approach and runway lighting, taxying techniques and the physiology of night flying. It wouldn't be a bad idea for you to get hold of one of these and read it before embarking on your night rating. The rating itself will certainly more than adequately reward you for the relatively small effort and expense that is involved in adding it to your PPL.

Instrument Flying

As a first aim after achieving their PPL many enterprising private pilots in the UK head for an IMC rating. The requirements for this are fairly stringent but not off-puttingly so. The achievement of an IMC rating is an indication that you have mastered a great deal of the advanced techniques of airmanship involved in flying light aircraft. The reward you get as the holder of a PPL with an IMC rating, is that you can legally continue flying in weather conditions that are poorer, in terms of cloud base and visibility, than the PPL holder without an IMC rating is allowed to penetrate. This rating can, in many ways, be regarded as an intermediate stage between the purely VFR PPL and a PPL with a full instrument rating (IR). Unfortunately, the IMC rating is valid only within UK airspace. Across the Channel or Irish Sea the holder of a UK PPL may not exercise the privileges of his or her IMC rating as this is not an internationally recognised rating.

The advantages of having an IMC rating whilst flying within UK airspace are significant, but still a long way below those of a full instrument rating. PPL pilots without an IMC rating are prohibited from flying outside controlled airspace when the visibility is less than 3km; IMC rated PPL pilots can fly outside controlled airspace down to zero visibility. Compared with the non-IMC rated PPL, the pilot with a valid IMC rating can also fly under IFR within Class D Airspace subject to certain specified minima. These limitations do tend to alter from time to time and so, rather than spell out the current ones here, when readers will probably find them misleading in a few months, I recommend that you always refer to the latest information that is available in publications such as the UK Air Pilot, CAP 53, current AICs, the ANO and elsewhere.

Before starting the course for an IMC rating a new PPL pilot must have flown at least 25 hours (which has to include a minimum of ten hours pilot in command and five hours cross-country flight) since applying for the PPL. To qualify for the IMC rating, a specified course which includes 15 hours of instrument flying (of which two may be conducted in a CAA approved simulator) must be completed. The associated ground study involves at least 20 hours of instruction covering physiological factors, flight instruments, the Aeronautical Information Service, flight planning and the privileges associated with the IMC rating. Finally a flight test and ground examination has to be passed. An IMC rating remains valid for 25 months, after which it can be renewed by issue of a certificate of competence on completion of a renewal flight test. The requirements involved are all detailed in CAP 53 and this publication really is required reading for any private pilot who is contemplating acquiring an IMC rating.

There has been much talk in connection with the harmonisation of regulations around Europe that the IMC rating, which as already mentioned is unique to the UK, might disappear unless the other JAR countries agree to accept it too. The current thinking appears to be that, although the other JAR countries seem to be unwilling to incorporate it into their systems, the IMC rating will still be retained by the UK authorities as an exception to the overall European standards. At the time of writing, there appears also to be a possibility that a modified version of the IMC rating, valid in other European countries, may be instituted under JAR.

Advantages of the IMC Rating

Quite apart from its usefulness in allowing a PPL holder to stay legal, within the UK at least, in weather conditions poorer than those in which unrated private pilots are permitted to fly, an IMC rating gives a pilot useful reassurance of his or her ability to fly accurately on instruments and to carry out a safe approach and landing using a precision or non-precision instrument landing system. It is an excellent confirmation of your ability to fly reasonably competently on instruments and it is a very useful insurance against being caught out by adverse weather conditions. Unfortunately it is as yet not valid Europe-wide, nor does it really give its holder any particularly significant advantages over the non-IMC PPL holder. It is, none the less, still a very useful and satisfying rating to acquire, either for its own sake or as a stepping stone towards the full IR.

The full instrument rating is a challenging step for any private pilot to take but it is, in the opinion of many pilots, a step that is essential unless you are prepared to limit the flying you do with your PPL solely to recreational flights or very limited business use. The reason for this thinking is simple. Weather conditions in the British Isles, and throughout much of continental Europe, are such that it is seldom possible to make a cross-country flight of any significant length and still be reasonably certain of being able to fly back again legally, keeping to your planned schedule, in weather conditions that comply with VFR. It is unfortunate that, in an effort to maintain a planned schedule, and with inadequate regard for the prevailing weather conditions, many private pilots without instrument ratings (and many of their passengers) have fallen victim to the fatal ailment sometimes referred to as 'get-home-itis'. One antidote for this nasty affliction is simply to have sufficient willpower to stay safely on the ground until conditions improve. Sadly, this simple remedy can sometimes have awkward side effects on business schedules or on personal plans. A less constricting cure for the malady is an adequate injection of instrument flying training. This, in conjunction with a suitably equipped aircraft, can render 'get-home-itis' relatively innocuous, but it still can remain a fatal disease for inexperienced pilots with Instrument Ratings who risk flying when more experienced IR qualified pilots would remain on the ground.

Unfortunately, the United Kingdom instrument rating is both expensive and difficult to achieve, especially for PPL pilots who fly only a limited number of hours annually. Before committing yourself to start training for an IR, desirable as it may be in terms of safety in every aspect of the flying you do, it is as well to analyse how the cost/benefit ratio would work out in your own circumstances. After a couple of experiences of sitting at some foreign airfield, socked-in by bad weather and burning with jealousy at the clever dicks who simply file IFR, fire up their engines and vanish through the layers of low cloud and rain, it is very tempting to decide you absolutely must head for an IR of your own. Life seems so much simpler for those other pilots, not having to phone up home or office to explain the situation, not running up unwanted hotel bills and aircraft parking charges. If you are ultimately aiming to qualify for a commercial licence then there is no question about it at all. An IR is an essential. If you are planning to use an aircraft regularly for business it is, to say the least, highly desirable. If you fly only for pleasure you may well find that, even after it becomes perfectly legal for you to fly in instrument conditions, your new instrument rating is very under utilised. For a whole variety of reasons, some of which are discussed below, many instrument rated private pilots often end up doing very little instrument flying at all.

Even so, the effort in self-improvement that you were involved in while qualifying for your instrument rating will certainly not have been in vain. An IR opens up all sorts of other opportunities, enabling you to fly airways in UK airspace (an activity incidentally, that you can undertake without any instrument qualification in many other parts of the world) gaining you valuable experience in controlled airspace operations, giving you an invaluable 'escape route' in case the weather clamps down on you unexpectedly, and generally increasing your flying experience and (hopefully) your weather wisdom. What an IR will not always do for you (contrary to the ideas nurtured by many non-instrument rated pilots) is make your flying simpler. It can at times actually make it considerably more complicated. Filing IFR may let you fly through clouds and along airways but it also means you have to ask for clearances to depart, to alter your routing and to change your cruising altitude. You lose much of the spontaneity that makes VFR flying so enjoyable. Nor does an IR make you magically independent of weather. Even airliners have to cancel occasionally, and they have certain advantages over you, like two pilots on the flight deck who are in regular flying practice, superior avionics to yours, de-icing equipment, ground support and so on.

IR doesn't make you Immune

Your aircraft is unlikely to be cleared for flight in known icing conditions. This cuts down considerably on cloud flying, especially (but not only) during the winter months. Even if you add an IR to your PPL this doesn't mean the end of weather imposed flight cancellations, even when there is no danger of encountering icing conditions. You still have weather minima; considerably lower than for the pilot without an

IR admittedly, but still high enough for you to be occasionally defeated by really grotty visibility or an awkwardly low cloud base. And an IR clipped to your PPL will definitely not guarantee you safe passage through a thunderstorm. What your IR does bring with it is a certainty that you are going to be called upon to make some very vital decisions. As a single pilot in a light aircraft with probably only limited avionics and instrumentation and no de-icing equipment, what degree of nasty weather are you prepared to tackle? You may have an IR in your pocket but are you not perhaps a little short of recent instrument flying experience? That's a point you should always factor into your go/no-go decision. When, as is often the case, the weather situation is not clear-cut, when the fog might or might not burn off, when the ceilings at the destination are hovering around your minima, the IR pilot can have quite a stressful time coming to a sensible decision. It can all be a whole lot more difficult for you than for the non-instrument rated PPL pilot alongside you.

Weighing the Cost

Think back over the last couple of years of your flying. How many times have you been held up by weather? How many times would you like to have flown but couldn't, simply because you were not instrument rated? How important these 'lost' flights, time delays and associated costs actually were to you, should give you at least a guide as to whether you should sign up for that IR course. If this approach seems to give you a green light, sit down next and add up the cost of the course at a CAA approved flying school. It involves at least 40 hours flying for an IR valid in single-engine aircraft, or 45 hours if you want a Group B IR for multi-engine aircraft. (Currently this could cost you anything from £5,000 to £7,500). Don't forget to include the costs of getting to and from wherever you will be doing the training, any accommodation expenses, the cost of your time away from work etc. Then there is the cost of the CAA Flight Examiner's Flight Test (currently a little over £500) and getting to Gatwick to sit the ground examinations which last about a day and a half. More time off work.

You, as a PPL pilot, have to meet precisely the same standards as any other CPL or ATPL applicant for an instrument rating. You are also required to go through the same regular re-testing to maintain the IR's validity. Financially, there are impilcations too. Is the aeroplane you intend flying correctly equipped and certified for IFR? If not, it might cost you quite a tidy sum to bring it up to standard, or considerably more to rent one which is fully IFR equipped. And of course, to make any real use of your IR you will need to subscribe to the appropriate *Jeppesen* or *Aerad* instrument charts and guides. These are quite a bit more expensive than the VFR flight guide and the half-mil ICAO charts which will no longer be sufficient for you as an instrument rated pilot.

If an honest appraisal of the financial situation persuades you that an IR is not for you, there is no need to be ashamed about it or to start making excuses. There are a multitude of other things still open for you to do with your PPL, and in some ways a decision not to go for an IR could well leave you with a more relaxed flying lifestyle. But if you can afford to become instrument rated, and the cost/benefit analysis indicates that in your case it is worth doing so, then you should certainly go for it. You then will be transformed into that pilot who can fly out of a sodden, dingy, grey airfield and leave the VFR pilots sitting waiting for a weather clearance. It is now you who will be able to spend the night at home with your family instead of in the airfield motel. You can experience the pleasure of leaving a miserable day on the ground and breaking out into sparkling sunshine a few thousand feet above ordinary mortals. You can enjoy the immense satisfaction of seeing the runway lights emerging from the overcast a few hundred feet below and ahead of you, just where the instruments told you they were going to be. You will have gained immeasurably in experience and competence from your extra training and this will have beneficial effects on many other aspects of your flying.

If your cash calculations show that an IR is likely to fit in with your flying lifestyle then that becomes the point where you have to make your first go/no-go decision. Whilst thinking of all the benefits that flying by instruments might bring, remember too what it is going to cost you in study, effort and hard cash before you finally make up your mind that this really is your thing.

Bigger, Faster and More Complex

Unless you happen to be a hopeless romantic about flying you have to agree that the real purpose of an aeroplane is to move people and goods around the place at a reasonable speed. Eventually (although some pilots never seem to reach this stage and others take ages to get there) you will probably realise that the leisurely speeds achieved by training and basic touring aircraft such as Cessna Skyhawks, Grumman Cheetahs and Piper Warriors, are less than ideal for much of the flying you would like to do. Aircraft like these, which once seemed to you to be a real handful to cope with, gradually begin to feel unexciting . . . and much too slow. The legs and wheels just hanging out there in the breeze begin to annoy you. You enviously watch other pilots take off in lean, mean machines that tuck their undercarriages away out of sight as soon as they are off the ground and benefit thereafter from increased speed, climb, and general efficiency. These are the signs that show you are beginning to suffer from the high performance syndrome.

Unless your basic training was rather unusual you probably did it on single engine light aircraft with fixed pitch propellers and fixed tricycle undercarriages, which were powered by piston engines that delivered not much more than 100 or 150 hp at the most. Your PPL, however, is a licence to pilot any aircraft of the type or group specified in your aircraft rating. For a private pilot the Group A rating specifies all single-engine aeroplanes not exceeding 5,700 kg maximum total weight authorised. A car driver who has just passed a driving test in a Ford Fiesta can, quite legally, hop into a Ferrari Testarossa and drive off in it. Similarly you, as holder of a brand-new UK PPL, are legally entitled to clamber into the cockpit of a Piper Malibu, or even a Supermarine Spitfire, and try to fly off in it. All you would have to do first would be to buy one, because that would probably be a whole lot easier than finding an owner of such an aircraft who is crazy enough to let you fly it. It has to be said too, that our hypothetical Ferrari driver would be much more likely to survive his terrestrial experience unscathed than you would your airborne adventure.

Not all aviation authorities take quite so lax an attitude as this. The FAA in the United States instituted a requirement back in 1973 that all pilots wanting to fly 'high performance' aircraft must take a one-time conversion course before they are permitted to fly an aircraft with either more than 200 horsepower, or a retractable undercarriage, controllable propeller and flaps. Strangely enough, under the FAA rules, one successful checkout with an FAA instructor in a 200 hp plane with fixed gear and fixed pitch prop, then entitles an American private pilot to fly a retractable with constant speed prop, so perhaps the FAA system isn't all that much more watertight than ours here in the UK. One could say that the authorities on both sides of the Atlantic have decided that it is just not possible to regulate good judgement into aviation, and that it is better to rely on the common sense of the pilots involved. They are also relying to some extent on the insurance under-writers who are justifiably reluctant to cover pilots, whose only experience is of flying aircraft like basic two-seat Cessnas, when they want to take over as pilots in command of sophisticated hot rod air-craft. Almost invariably the insurers insist on being satisfied that such pilots have first undergone adequate supervised conversion training.

Making Conversions
So, if and when you do decide to head for more power, more aero-dynamic efficiency or probably both together, what sort of conversion

training should you be looking for? Most reasonably competent pilots could probably rely on their basic piloting instinct to cope with a moderate increase above the horsepower they have been accustomed to, if that is the only change. They, and you, could quickly adjust to the aircraft's greater tendency to swing more as you take-off and to the way it climbs more quickly and generally makes everything happen a little more rapidly than you have become accustomed to.

Moving to an aircraft that has something more than just a few extra horses to pull it along, one that also has a retractable undercarriage, constant speed propeller and perhaps a fuel-injected engine, is a different matter entirely. With no training or experience of constant speed propeller operation it is not at all difficult, even for a pilot with many hours of fixed pitch prop flying in the log book, to inflict some potentially expensive loads on the innards of the engine. This type of prop can be regarded as acting in a manner similar to the gearbox of a car. Select fine pitch (or low gear) and you get high RPM for take-off. Changing into a 'second gear' provides a suitable setting for climbing, and coarse pitch (high gear) is what should normally be used for economical cruising with the engine turning at low RPM. Trying to pull away at full throttle from slow speed in a car with top or overdrive gear selected, results in the engine 'lugging' and 'pinking' and gives pretty lamentable performance. Trying to fly an aircraft at low airspeed with coarse pitch and full throttle you don't hear the pinking, but it (and the resulting damage to the engine) is still liable to be taking place and the performance is equally awful. Before each reduction of RPM (coarser pitch selection) the throttle, which is still the power control, must be moved to a lower power setting so that the slower revving engine will not be 'lugging' with the throttle too wide open. To ensure that the engine is ready to respond to full throttle in the event of an overshoot from a balked landing, the propeller control must always be in the fine (high RPM) position before landing.

Rather than simply trying to memorise blindly which it is of the pitch and throttle levers you should move first when increasing and when decreasing power (rev up; throttle back) it is far better to take a bit of time to understand what each lever does and how this affects the workings of the engine. There are many good textbooks on the subject and it is too involved for us to go into in detail here. It is however worth mentioning one benefit that a real understanding of this subject should bring for you. It should help dispel one of aviation's many myths. The one about 'squaring' the engine settings. Put about by many instructors who are either trying to make life over simple for their students, or who (less charitably) have probably never troubled to learn the subject thoroughly themselves, this is the idea that you must never have the manifold pressure (measured in inches of mercury) exceeding the RPM (measured in hundreds of RPM). They affirm that the ideal situation is always to set the throttle to give, say, 27 inches manifold pressure when the revs are 2700 (for take-off), 25 'squared' for the climb and perhaps 23 'squared' in the cruise. It is difficult to understand where this myth originated since, as any engineer will confirm, manifold pressure and engine RPM are like chalk and cheese, apples and oranges. Some instructors, and a whole lot of experienced pilots of high performance aircraft, even go so far as to suggest that if the inches of mercury ever do exceed the hundreds of RPM, you are overboosting the engine and it is liable to disintegrate. The fact is that with a normally aspirated engine, you cannot overboost it. Such engines cannot use any pressure other than ambient atmospheric pressure to bring air into the cylinders. Aircraft manuals and POHs don't use the term overboost; many in fact list normal approved ranges of manifold pressure and RPM settings which include such combinations as 25 inches and 2100 RPM. It is only if you are willing to learn how to handle these engine control levers correctly that you will be able to maximise the performance, and really justify the extra cost involved in flying high performance aircraft. Manufacturers who write these handbooks generally know more about their aircraft and engines than instructors who have been too idle to read the manuals so that they can teach students correctly. The moral of this is, once again, always to read, learn and digest the information in the POH or aircraft manual . . . and not to accept as gospel all that comes out of an instructor's mouth.

Remember The Greens

In a high performance aircraft one omission from your before landing checks could easily result in a financially disastrous wheels-up contact with the runway. It is all too easy, following years of mumbling the amusing 'undercarriage down and welded' as part of the downwind check in a simple aircraft, to absent-mindedly mumble the same phrase when you are flying a retractable. Not all of these are kind enough to warn you automatically of your oversight in the way the Piper Arrow kindly does. Folding legs and wheels come in a multiplicity of different designs. Some, such as Mooneys, Bonanzas and the Comanche, use electric motors and reduction gearing to operate the undercarriage. The majority, however, use hydraulic power for this job. Some older types of aircraft use engine-driven hydraulic pumps but the most popular system in current designs is electrohydraulic. The Piper Arrow is typical of these. It has a power pack located under the rear seats. This comprises an electric motor coupled to a hydraulic pump and a reservoir of hydraulic oil. After take-off, moving the gear switch from down to up once you have established a positive rate of climb, earths one side of the electric motor's relay. The current coming to the other side from the aircraft main power bus-bar has first to pass through a couple of circuit-breakers. One of these is designed so that no current is allowed to pass any time there is any weight on the undercarriage; this prevents inadvertent retraction whilst the aircraft is on the ground. The other is controlled by a hydraulic pressure switch which allows current to flow if the system pressure drops below about 1,000 psi and cuts it off if it exceeds about 1,500 psi. The purpose behind this is to let the motor run and the pump force oil into the cylinders that retract the undercarriage, until all three legs and wheels are safely tucked away. The system pressure will then rise as the motor pump unit tries to push more oil into the now stationary system and, when pressure exceeds 1,500 psi, this second pressure switch cuts the motor out. If the pressure later falls below the 1,000 psi figure it automatically switches itself on again for long enough to build up pressure again, ensuring that the wheels stay safely in place. The Gear Down switch more or less reverses the process, with the electric motor and pump turning in the other direction. It doesn't have to work quite so hard since gravity lends a hand in this direction. The 'Gear Unsafe' or red/green lights are coupled to microswitches in the undercarriage system.

Most retractables also have an emergency undercarriage lowering system available, in case there is ever a failure of the normal system. These vary in operation, and are fortunately not all that often used, but you should always ensure that you are familiar with precisely how the one on the aircraft you are flying does operate. You never know just when you might need the knowledge. A failure usually means that the aircraft is turned into a fixed gear model, because not many manufacturers explain how to use any form of emergency retraction, only extension. Most Cessna systems do in fact permit emergency retraction, although the handbooks don't usually explain how to use them for this purpose. After all, once you have got a defective undercarriage down into place for landing, it doesn't seem altogether a bad idea just to leave it there rather than tempt fate, would you not agree?

Just like the flaps (and indeed the aircraft themselves) retractable undercarriages have limiting speeds of their own. These are determined by several factors, the main one often being the strength of the undercarriage doors and their ability to stay attached to the airframe. V_{lo} is the maximum speed at which the landing gear may be raised or lowered and on some aircraft another slightly higher speed is quoted, V_{le} which is the maximum speed you may fly with the landing gear locked down in the extended position. Some models also have a maximum gear retraction speed, lower than the V_{lo}. Taking the Piper Arrow as an example again, you can lower the wheels at the V_{lo} of 133 knots, but the handbook quotes 111 knots as the maximum airspeed for retraction of the undercarriage. Whichever type you are flying, these are speeds you must know. Without them at your fingertips you are putting the structural integrity of the aircraft at risk.

If the aircraft's engine is fuel-injected, and until now you've always flown carburetter types, you might end up with nothing worse than a flat battery and a red face when you discover you have no idea how to get the thing to start; at least that might save you from some other embarrassments! High performance aeroplanes also tend to be fitted with avionics stacks that are a bit more comprehensive than training aircraft usually have. It is well worth spending some time on the ground studying the knobs and switches associated with these before even thinking about flying. Trying to work out in the air how to change from VHF Box 1 to Box 2, or how to set a particular code on a transponder you aren't familiar with, is a problem you can do without. This sort of trivial but mind occupying thing can quickly get inexperienced pilots into trouble while scudding through the air at a speed that is appreciably faster than they are accustomed to.

Each Step Seems Smaller
Moving from a Cessna 152 to a 172 Skyhawk is a comparatively tiny change in techniques and procedures; the change from the 172 to a 177RG Cardinal requires considerably more preparation. But once you have made one such transition, whether to a Cardinal RG, a Beech Bonanza, Piper Arrow, TB-20 Trinidad or a SIAI-Marchetti SF-260, then you should have developed the basic background knowledge that will allow you to make the conversion more easily to other similar (or even quite different) high performance or complex aircraft. All you should need to do then is simply to use your own intelligence and common sense and to study the appropriate aircraft manuals thoroughly before you get into the cockpit.

Familiarity Breeds Competence
Studying the manual is an important prerequisite for any conversion onto a new type; it is especially important when you are making that big step to your first high performance machine. Read the handbook, memorise it as far as you can, sleep with the damn thing, get someone to quiz you on it until you know the systems, performance, limitations, emergency procedures and all the rest that there is to know about it. Time spent on the ground doing this, whether at home or in the classroom, is cheap; time spent airborne learning the same stuff in the cockpit can work out pretty expensive. Knowing in advance the

different procedures that have to be used to start a cold engine and a hot one can save embarrassment. Knowing before you ever touch the controls how to operate the emergency landing gear extension system can save more than that. Keeping the fuel tanks in balance is no problem in a Cessna 152; it can be much more complicated, and is also much more important, in many other types. Just because you have more power up front still doesn't necessarily mean you can now carry four up, plus full tanks and baggage, without going outside weight and balance limits. Learn what these limits are for the new type you are going to fly. If this is the first time you have met a constant speed propeller, that is another whole field of study for you to absorb before you even touch either the throttle or the pitch lever. Remember which of them it is you do move first and why.

The basic rule is a simple one. Know your aeroplane. Know what to expect, know what to do if something unexpected happens. It is all that much easier too, if you take the trouble to understand why things work the way they do. This is not the book to explain fully the interaction between cylinder pressure and propeller pitch, what makes a fuel-injected engine start differently from the carburetter types you are used to, why there are different maximum speeds for retracting and extending the undercarriage. There are plenty of good textbooks that will explain these matters to you. Take the trouble to read and understand them, ensure you have extracted all there is to know from the aircraft's own handbook, and you should approach your first flight in the high performance aeroplane with a great deal more confidence. You should also succeed in flying it a great deal more competently than the know-all who mutters something about them all being much the same as, he or she climbs into the cockpit and starts the slow and expensive job of learning everything from scratch the hard way. Know your aeroplane thoroughly on the ground before you start getting to know it in the air.

During my own conversion to the first high performance type I flew, my instructor insisted that I sit in the cockpit with my eyes blindfolded and reach out instantaneously to touch or point to each control or instrument the moment he named it. Flap lever; oil temperature; fire extinguisher; VHF radio; landing lamp; rudder trim; turn and slip; hood release. I can still hear his litany ... and even four decades after last flying one of them I can still remember where most of these things are in the cockpit of a Harvard!

Taking to the Air
With these ground study preliminaries all safely out of the way, it is time to start making your transition to a high performance aircraft in the air. Keeping up with the new type is a common problem for the tyro

pilot; everything seems to be happening a lot quicker than it used to do in a simpler, slower type like a Cessna 152, Piper Tomahawk or Robin DR400. You must always remember that it is you who are flying the aeroplane; don't ever begin to let it fly you. The moment you start getting the feeling that the aeroplane is trying to take control is the moment to stop, hand over to the instructor if necessary, get a grip of the situation and begin again. In some ways high performance aircraft are actually easier to fly, once you get used to them, than the lighter types because of their heavier wing loading. This tends to make them more stable, but that can be a drawback too, as it gives them a tendency to fly themselves straight into the ground if you let yourself get behind the aeroplane on the approach. It also gives many complex aircraft very different stall characteristics from the ones you have grown used to on training aircraft. Some, especially when in the flaps extended and gear down landing configuration, have the particularly nasty habit of giving the pilot virtually no buffeting, or any other stall warning at all, before everything suddenly goes horribly pear-shaped.

Circuits are the Hardest Bits

It is while you are flying circuits that the extra workload and higher performance of these machines might first tend to make you feel that the aeroplane is getting ahead of you. More rudder is needed to keep straight on take-off due to the extra engine torque. Then there is the gear to be retracted and next it takes a few seconds longer to make the adjustment to climb power, since there are now two controls to be adjusted, and meantime the higher rate of climb means you are up to circuit height appreciably sooner than you are accustomed to in a more leisurely aeroplane. The downwind leg should take about the same time as usual, because you should reduce power (two controls again) to adjust your speed to keep pace with trainers in the circuit. That slower downwind helps too, because there are a few extra items (such as the little matter of wheels) to include in the downwind checks. I still find the old BUMPFFHH a good mnemonic for a downwind checklist, well suited to most aircraft. Brakes off; Undercarriage down; Mixture fully rich; Prop pitch set to fine (high revs) unless for noise considerations you prefer to leave that to short final; Flaps set appropriately; Fuel on correct tank with booster pump on; Hood locked and Harness tight. The next power reduction, probably to about 10 or 12 inches of manifold pressure, follows quickly, then base leg, check the green lights to indicate the wheels really are down and locked, speed checked to the book figure for approach. On final approach full flap is needed to reduce speed to $1.3V_{so}$ and your power setting should be adequate to achieve a stabilised approach with a sink speed of no more than 500 feet per minute. More than that and the higher wing loading is liable to make the aeroplane fail to respond to the flare and thump down hard onto the runway. This type of aircraft is seldom flown power off on the approach because the increased wing loading would make a glide approach very much shorter and steeper than a similar approach on a simple touring or training aircraft.

Getting Checked Out

The first time you make the transition to a high performance single engine aeroplane it is well worth spending several hours in general handling and circuit work, accompanied by a pilot (preferably an instructor) experienced on the type. The time to discontinue the conversion training will become obvious to yourself; it is once you know you can keep comfortably ahead of the aeroplane under all circumstances. If you haven't learned how to stay ahead of the machine you are supposed to be controlling, you really still amount to no more than the proverbial accident waiting for somewhere to happen.

Whilst converting to a higher performance aircraft you are, of course, improving your general airmanship and flying skills for simpler aircraft at the same time. And when the time comes to move on to cope with a different high performance aeroplane, even though you shouldn't require anything like as much conversion, it is still a wise move to arrange another short checkout. This should help to ensure that you are familiar with any particular quirks the aeroplane may have before you set off to fly it. Much better than being surprised by them, up in the air, all on your own.

Flying high performance aircraft is not necessarily an end in itself. All knowledge is cumulative and what you have learned in converting forces you to think farther ahead simply because everything is happening that much faster. This will be of enormous help to you later if you decide to go on to learn to fly multi-engine aircraft or to train for an instrument rating.

Taming Taildraggers

Not until several years after World War 2 ended did many pilots do their primary training on anything other than tailwheel aircraft. After initial training on Tiger Moths, Magisters, Cornells and Piper Cubs, some WW2 pilots had to convert onto tricycle gear aircraft like the Airacobra, Mitchell, Albemarle, Liberator or Lightning, but it wasn't until jet fighters like the Messerschmitt 262 Schwalbe, Gloster Meteor and de Havilland Vampire came along that nosewheel aircraft began to appear in large numbers.

Postwar basic training continued mainly on Piper Cubs and Pacers, Cessna 140s, Tiger Moths, Chipmunks and similar tailwheel types. Until Piper brought out the nosewheel version of the Pacer in 1951, and called it the Tripacer, about the only nosewheel light aircraft seen in any numbers had been the Ercoupe. The Tripacer sold like hot cakes and suddenly everyone found out what they had been missing. Cessna soon caught on to the idea of tricycle gear light aircraft; the result was the 1955 Cessna 172, closely followed by the Cessna 182. Except for the Tipsy Nipper, Bölkow Junior and Rallye, European light plane manu-facturers remained loyal to tailwheels until towards the end of the 1950s, but since then more and more pilots have learned to fly without ever experiencing the trials and tribulations of pulling off a smooth, neat, three-point landing in a tailwheel aircraft. Nowadays a light aircraft with its nose in the air and tail on the ground looks a little odd, something of an anachronism, and a sort of mystique has grown up around these oddball machines.

Nosewheel trained pilots are sometimes told they'll never be real pilots until they have learned to cope with one of these relics from a bygone age. Some accept the challenge and find out that they do indeed have quite a lot new to learn. Others retort, 'Why should I bother with a tailwheel aircraft? What possible advantage is there in that old-fashioned idea?' And in a way they are quite correct. Taildragger aficionados will run out of reasons after saying that taildraggers are lighter, less draggy, give better prop clearance and are generally better for short, rough strips. They keep quiet about the swing on take-off, poor forward visibility on the ground, difficulty of consistently landing smoothly and the always-lurking danger of a ground loop. But they still love their aircraft, the same way other folk love a manual camera instead of an automatic one, a fountain pen instead of a ballpoint, a manual gearbox in a car rather than an automatic transmission.

Learning to cope with a taildragger is still a worthwhile extension of any pilot's skill and one that can be accomplished by any competent pilot without having to spend too much cash in the process. It is also a prerequisite for any pilot wanting to fly a Formula 1 racer, a biplane, almost any warbird, glider tug or crop-sprayer, many aerobatic aircraft, lots of PFA homebuilt types or any open cockpit aeroplane, since practically all of these are tailwheel designs. Pilots who can only cope with tricycle undercarriage aircraft severely limit the range of interesting aeroplanes they can fly. Before signing up for a few conver-sion lessons at one of the specialist schools or clubs offering instruction in Tiger Moths, Piper Cubs, Jodels, Stampes and even tailwheel Cessna

150s (these organisations are all listed annually in for example *Pilot* Magazine's April *Where to Fly Directory*) it is as well to have an idea of where the main differences lie.

In the tricycle undercarriage machines you have been flying up till now, the centre of gravity (C of G) is in front of the main undercarriage wheels. It obviously must be since if it wasn't the nosewheel would never stay on the ground! And equally obviously, a tailwheel aircraft's C of G has to be aft of the main wheels, otherwise it would come to rest with its prop digging into the turf instead of having its little tailwheel sitting safely on the ground. In the air this generally makes not the slightest bit of difference, but on the ground it certainly does. In a tricycle machine, the forward C of G position helps to pull the aircraft back into line if it becomes displaced from a straight line while decelerating during the landing run. In the taildragger it has exactly the opposite effect, pushing from behind the main gear and tending to swing the tail around in front of the main wheels – the classic ground loop situation. Taken to its extreme, if not corrected by a careful jab of opposite brake, closure of the throttle and holding the stick fully back and into the turn, the tail can swing around in a full circle, a wing and maybe a wheel may rise, then the tail can lift off the ground and (if the panic-stricken pilot slams on the anchors) the aircraft can even flip onto its back. All of which is most undignified. Yet after a little proper tuition it is totally unnecessary, and not all that likely to happen, despite all the hangar flying tales you hear about ground looping.

Nosewheel aircraft are designed so that they are almost in flying attitude while on the ground, requiring only slight rotation at the correct speed in order to take off. Taildraggers, on the other hand, have props that point at a distinct angle into the air whilst static, and they all require to have their tails raised prior to take-off. This has the important consequence that, in addition to the slipstream effect and torque effect that tend to swing tricycle undercarriage aircraft on take-off, taildragger pilots also have to contend with the gyroscopic effect (caused by tilting the rotating propeller as the tail comes up) and asymmetric blade effect (the result of the down-going prop blade cutting into the air at a greater angle of attack than the up-going one). The fact that all four of these forces happen to act in the same direction means that tailwheel aircraft have an appreciably greater tendency to swing on take-off. This is a swing to the left with clockwise rotating engines (all American ones) and to the right on those few aircraft fitted with counter-clockwise rotating engines, mainly the older European manufactured ones like the Gipsy, Cirrus, Renault and so on.

In the heyday of tailwheel aircraft most flying took place from grass airfields and the duty runway always pointed more or less straight into wind. With no crosswinds to contend with, swings that led to ground loops were comparatively rare occurrences. The ability to cope with crosswind landings in a tailwheel aircraft is one sign of a well-trained pilot who has kept in good practice. The personal satisfaction obtained from being able to make consistently smooth and accurate three-point landings in a taildragger, is just one of the many joys you can achieve from being a pilot. Landing tail high on the main wheels only, is another technique worth learning; it helps you cope with crosswinds and gusty conditions. If you were taught to fly on a tricycle undercarriage aeroplane you will undoubtedly have fond memories of the thrill you got from your first solo flight in it. You could well find that your first solo at the controls of a tailwheel aeroplane will give you just as much pleasure, and maybe even more satisfaction, when you conclude it with a sweet, smooth greaser of a three-point landing.

Having mastered the quirks of flying taildraggers you'll find that many new aspects of flying have opened up to you. As already mentioned, the best aerobatic aircraft tend to have tailwheels. So do many of the economical microlights and rugged types of aircraft that are best suited to short strips. You will have the satisfaction of knowing that you have learned to fly the way every pilot had to learn throughout powered flying's first half-century. The tailwheel training and experience should have turned you into a more competent and a more confident pilot, even when you are piloting one of these newfangled things with the wheel at the sharp end that take most of the airmanship and half the fun out of landing in stiff crosswinds.

Techniques for Twins

In the United States one of the most popular additions to a private pilot licence is a multi-engine rating. However, the same cannot be said for Europe in general. Differing costs of hire and ownership of twin-engine aircraft, higher operating costs due to greedier fuel burn and landing charge penalties, tend to put even the smaller light twins out of reach of many European pilots, however desirable they might at first appear to be. None the less, the training involved in learning how to fly a multi-engine aircraft is valuable experience and none of the techniques to be tackled are beyond the ability of any competent single-engine private pilot. Transition from single-engine piloting to flying twins is, of course, an essential early step for any pilot making his or her way towards a commercial licence.

Buying Safety?

On the face of things, a twin-engine aircraft should be a safer machine for you to fly than a single, especially if much of your flying is to be done over the sea or inhospitable terrain. If the motor quits in a single, there is only one way to go, and that is down. In a twin, theoretically at least, the loss of one engine should be no big deal. The other engine will continue to power the aircraft as the pilot flies happily on to a suitable place for landing. But to achieve this ideal state of affairs that pilot has to be properly trained, in practice, and on top of his or her job. Even then, things aren't always quite as straightforward as that. For a start several light twins are scarcely able to maintain height on one engine when heavily loaded, at high density altitude, or when in take-off or landing configuration. Unfortunately, most of the types that are likely to seem almost affordable for you, either to own or rent, fall into this category; the Piper Seminole, Seneca I and Twin Comanche, the Beech Duchess, Grumman Cougar and a good few others. The pilot's operating handbook figures may tell a different story, quoting quite an impressive single-engine service ceiling figure. What they don't usually make clear is that in order to climb up to that ceiling the aircraft must be 'clean' (with wheels and flaps up) atmospheric conditions must be normal and the dead engine's propeller must be feathered. With a windmilling engine, wheels and/or flaps out in the slipstream, a light twin with one engine out becomes a very inefficient flying machine. It is sometimes not much more performance-wise than a glider with a mechanical source of noise out on one wing. The smallest of the 'real' twin-engine aircraft, which are really capable of maintaining height and even climbing on one engine, are the Beech Baron, Cessna 310 and the Piper Aztec.

The reason for the poor performance of some light twins with one engine isn't difficult to figure out. Supposing a hypothetical light twin requires 160 horsepower to fly straight and level in its minimum drag configuration, and that it is fitted with two 200 horsepower engines. It obviously has 240 spare horses to give it an impressive rate of climb and a useful cruising speed. If one of the engines fails, however, only 40 horsepower remains surplus to ideal minimum drag cruise requirements. That is quickly absorbed by a windmilling propeller and the hefty bootful of rudder you need to keep the aircraft straight, never mind any additional drag from wheels or flaps. So down it goes, not quite so rapidly perhaps as a single-engine aircraft under similar circumstances, but inexorably down. And the twin pilot is left with a considerably increased workload compared with the single-engine jockey after his or her motor quits. There is the asymmetric thrust of the remaining good engine to fight, the dead prop to feather, the systems of a more complex machine to cope with, and he or she is still confronted with an inevitable forced landing to be planned for at the same time. All this will give you some idea of why the multi-engine qualification usually takes a competent single-engine private pilot at least ten flying hours to complete (probably costing well over half what you paid for your entire PPL course). It shows too, how learning to fly twins will polish up virtually any pilot's level of general airmanship.

A Cessna 310 costs approximately three times as much per hour to hire as a Cessna 152, so it behoves the multi-engine student to minimise the time spent in the air learning things that could just as easily have been learned on the ground. For the sake of your bank balance, plan on spending at least six hours on serious book study before each hour in the cockpit. This study will cover the numerous V-speeds that affect twins and not singles; V_{mc}, V_{xse}, V_{yse} and so on, what the 'critical engine' is, and the nuts and bolts of how you feather an engine (and how to be absolutely positive that it is the correct engine you are feathering!). It would also be stupid to embark on twin training if you have never learned how to fly any single-engine aircraft more complex than fixed undercarriage, fixed prop trainers and tourers. That way you end up paying around three times as much as you need to, just to learn how to cope with retractable gear, constant speed propellers and higher than normal wing-loading. Best get all that behind you first whilst piloting a less expensive high performance single.

Single-engine Twin Training

Most of your training for the multi-engine rating will be spent with only one of your engines delivering power. With both engines in good nick, apart from the slightly busier looking cockpit, you'll find there is precious little difference between piloting the twin and flying the single engine machines you are more accustomed to. There are differences though. One you will very quickly notice, is the lack of useful screws, rivets and scratch marks on the engine cowling ahead of you that you have been in the habit of using, perhaps subconsciously, to line up with the runway on landing. Once they stuck an engine out on each wing most designers decided that a stubby little short nose was all you needed in front of the cockpit, and you just have to get used to the change in runway sight pictures that this brings. The fact that the port engine looks bigger to you (ensconced as you are in the left-hand seat) than the starboard, stuck away out there on the far wing, brings problems on landing too. Instinct tells you to try to even things up, the result of which can be your swinging the aircraft to the left before touchdown, with an accompanying squeal of protest from the tyres. The greater curvature that the average twin's windshield has, also tends to distort your picture of the runway; yet another small item you have to become accustomed to. And these small items do tend to add up.

Only the first hour or so of your multi-engine training will be spent getting the feel of the machine with both donkeys pulling; turning it, stalling it, feeling its slow-flying characteristics and becoming accustomed to the new appearance of the world when it is no longer seen through that familiar propeller disc. From there on you will get to know in a very practical way the meaning of the word 'asymmetric'. Shortly thereafter you are liable to become very aware of a certain group of muscles in your legs after you have spent many happy hours having one engine or the other 'failed' on you. This exercise has just one aim; that is to enable you to develop the essential art of controlling a twin that has suddenly become a single-engine aeroplane, just in case one that you are flying ever decides to pull that trick on you. You will learn a new V-speed here. V_{mc}, the minimum control speed which is, in effect, the lowest speed at which you can keep the nose straight with one engine out of action. This actually is a variable quantity, depending on the weight of the aircraft, which engine is out, whether the dead prop is feathered etc and even a few intangibles such as pilot technique. Twins bring lots of interesting new V-speeds for you to learn. One of the most useful is V_{sse}, the safe single-engine speed, which is the slightly higher minimum speed that you should substitute for V_{mc} during engine failure training. This might help to reduce the too frequent accidents that have occurred when an over optimistic low V_{mc} has been used. One of the least useful must surely be V_{xse}; this is the best angle of climb speed when flying with one engine dead. Under what set of circumstances can you envisage trying to clear an obstacle in a twin with only one fan turning?

Like most steps up the ladder of pilot proficiency, being able to exercise the privileges of a multi-engine rating can bring a great deal of satisfaction. Perhaps not least among these is the satisfaction of being able to explain to those lesser mortals who are still restricted to single engine aircraft, just how easy it all really was, how much more fun it is to fly a big twin (like a Cougar or Twin Comanche perhaps?) and how much safer it is for all on board when you wing your way off to Guernsey or Rotterdam. (Cross your fingers as you make that claim, though; better not to put the theory and your own new prowess to the test, especially if the aircraft is anywhere near maximum gross). There is something about flying a twin that does strange things to the ego of some pilots. These aircraft seem to give them a feeling of prestige that is quite liable to lead to a bad dose of over-confidence. If you were born under one of the star signs that makes you susceptible to this, do your best to guard against it.

What really makes flying twins more fun is the very fact that they are more complicated than your average single. The feeling that you have the competence to master all these electric, hydraulic, fuel (up to six tanks to juggle on some) and other systems can give you a real feeling of satisfaction. There is possibly a slight danger that, as a new twin pilot, you may develop delusions of grandeur. These are sometimes fed by ATC's tendency to accord some priority to twins over single-engine aircraft. Some controllers seem to reckon that if you fly a twin you must be important. There is no doubt that, as and when you return to fly a humble single again, you are going to miss that feeling of superiority.

There is yet another problem that you might meet unless you own or have a share in the twin you intend to fly. Some insurance companies are not at all happy about pilots with minimal multi-engine experience and this can make it difficult to find a twin to hire, and thus ever manage to log the experience in twins that is necessary to hire one. Catch 22 for the newly fledged twin-engine pilot. It can be an enormous help in this situation if you have a friend who is prepared (or who might be persuaded) to let you put in some P2 time in the right-hand seat of a multi-engine aircraft until the hours totals in the multi-engine columns of your logbook look less meagre. Once you have amassed around 25 to 30 hours of multi-engine time it should prove easier to find suitable aircraft available for you to hire.

A twin-engine aircraft appears at first to offer enhanced safety compared with a single, especially for night and over-water flying, but this can be somewhat illusory unless the pilot is right in top form and the circumstances (and aircraft) are favourable. Conversion to twins is the logical and necessary step up from single-engine flying for all budding CPLs, but it actually offers fewer real benefits to the private flyer than might initially appear. And it doesn't come cheap. For the average private pilot, who doesn't have unlimited funds at his or her disposal, nor serious aspirations in the direction of owning a twin, there are probably better ways of breaking new ground before deciding to master the art of multi-engine flying.

Loops, Rolls, Aresti and the Rest

The old saw about one person's meat being another person's poison is certainly very applicable to the gentle art of aerobatics. To some pilots the delight that can be obtained from pirouetting around the sky in a series of simple loops and rolls, or from performing a choreography of complex aerobatic manoeuvres, is something that borders on the ecstatic. Many other pilots have a total aversion to the idea of throwing themselves about the heavens in an aeroplane; the very thought of positive and negative g-forces, of seeing the earth rotate around them and occasionally even appear somewhere down above their heads, fills them with revulsion.

I was introduced to aerobatics in rather an uncivilised way. On my very first flight as a student pilot, after about half an hour of a lesson termed 'air experience and the effects of controls' my over-exuberant RAF instructor suddenly said 'Now you'd like to find out what a loop's like', and without any further ado he put the nose of the Miles Magister into what seemed to me a potentially lethal downward angle while my stomach rose into my gullet. Mother earth then vanished altogether, my guts lurched violently down, the landscape came into view again somewhere above my head and everything went very quiet for a moment before it seemed to me we were again suicidally diving straight down to meet the ground. 'D'ya like that, eh?' I heard. I swallowed back a mouthful of bile and lied through my teeth, 'Yes, it was great', whilst praying inwardly that he wouldn't treat me to any more nonsense like that.

A somewhat thoughtless demonstration like that has put many people off aerobatics for life. Fortunately for me however, other instructors later took the time to explain in advance what was involved in each manoeuvre, then demonstrated loops and rolls, followed me through on the controls and finally let me off solo to throw my aeroplane around the sky. I never achieved a level of aerobatic prowess that would have enabled me to take part in it as a competitive sport, but I did at least experience the thrills of coaxing Tiger Moths around slow rolls without falling out of the sky, and later enjoyed the extra performance of the Chipmunk which made all the standard manoeuvres seem that bit easier. Then I had the pleasure of taking Harvards around sequences of aerobatics; that redoubtable machine may now look like an ancient lumbering monster but it is a delightfully agile aeroplane to fly. My most vivid memories of past aerobatic pleasures come from the all too short spell I was lucky enough to spend as a jet fighter pilot. The Gloster Meteor F4's twin jet engines didn't give it the thrust-to-weight ratio of later fighters, but for RAF pilots in the 1950s it marked a quantum step in performance, enabling us to twist the world around our aircraft in ways that had never before been possible.

Keeping Within Limits

As a civilian PPL flying for your own pleasure you will probably never be able to sample the joys of jet fighter aerobatics but that doesn't by any means imply that for you to take some aerobatic training would be a waste of either your time or effort. There is a great deal of fun to be had from even something as simple as a Cessna 152 Aerobat and, if the aerobatic aspect of aviation really begins to take your fancy, there are many other more agile aircraft than Cessnas easily available for PPL pilots to fly: old-timers like Stampes, Moths and Bückers; cheap to fly PFA types such as the Tipsy Nipper or the Hyperbipe; expense no object machines like warbirds and of course the specialist aerobatic aircraft like Zlins, Extras and Pitts Specials. The Chipmunk, Beagle Pup and Slingsby T67 also are all excellent machines in which you can learn the basic manoeuvres. But you should never ever attempt to fly aerobatics in a standard aeroplane. Light aircraft aren't built like battleships. They are designed to meet certain certification standards and if you exceed their design load factor this can result in permanent structural damage, even if nothing obvious appears to have fallen asunder. Any overstrain of that nature can sometimes come to light only much later, when some unsuspecting pilot (possibly yourself) hits some severe turbulence for example, and experiences a structural failure all because some ass had tried to show off as a smart aerobatic pilot in a non-aerobatic aeroplane. Oh yes, I agree you probably have seen some pretty impressive manoeuvres performed at air shows in seriously non-aerobatic aircraft, but these were being done by expert pilots who had learned the manoeuvres in structurally strong, aerobatic aircraft, and who were making absolutely sure that the stress limits on the standard machine were not being exceeded. Normal aerobatic loops, rolls and stall turns, properly executed, are well within the strength limitations of lots of standard aeroplanes; the problems are liable to come when some pilot makes a slight mistake and the manoeuvre doesn't go quite as intended. Then it is all too easy to put loads on airframes and engines that are far in excess of their normal design and certification limits. Being aware that such dangers exist, and knowing how to combat them, is all part of learning aerobatics. It is not a bad maxim to remember that if something starts to go wrong when you are part way through a manoeuvre, things are more probably going to get worse rather than better unless you do something positive about it.

Quite apart from the sheer exhilaration involved in flying aerobatics (immensely important though that is to all enthusiastic aerobatic pilots) just learning how to perform them is also going to improve your overall flying ability. The coordination, the timing and judgement required, the self-discipline needed to maintain safety at all times and the need for you to stay in reasonable physical shape yourself all help to produce a general sharpening up of your everyday piloting skills.

Since spinning ceased to be a compulsory part of the PPL course in the UK many pilots have been let loose in the skies with no experience of anything other than relatively straight and level flight, with just the occasional steep turn and an odd stall and recovery. The very ladylike way that many training aircraft stall these days too, means that many of these pilots have no real experience of how an aeroplane responds and how it should be handled if it gets into an unusual attitude. There is no point in saying you are never going to get your aircraft into such a situation; you may have precious little choice in the matter. One day you may be flung around like a leaf in a storm by lee wave turbulence while flying over mountains, or perhaps you will have your aircraft picked up and tossed like a toy by the gust front associated with a thunderstorm. Even if the air traffic controller gives you the full time interval on the approach after a heavy aircraft has landed, that is no absolute guarantee that an unseen wake vortex might not still be lurking by the runway to flick you half-over onto your back. If throughout your flying life you have never been in an aeroplane in an attitude such as that, you will be considerably less likely to know how to recover safely from it than would a pilot with some experience of aerobatics.

Getting ready

Aerobatic experience is not something you should try to gain on your own; not initially at least. Many of the books about aerobatics do make some of the manoeuvres sound fairly straightforward, but there are traps for the unwary. Falling into some of these traps can wreak havoc with airframes and engines, not to mention pilots. No; your first venture into the world of aerobatics really must be in a suitable aerobatic aircraft and in the company of an experienced aerobatic instructor. Until your instructor has gone through the basics with you and declared you fit to go and polish up your performance of loops, rolls and the rest on your own, please don't risk your aircraft and your neck by 'having a little go at it' by yourself.

There aren't any special requirements in the way of equipment or clothing laid down for aerobatic flying, but it is only sensible to be appropriately clad for the job. It is bad practice whilst aerobatting to hang on to the control column (or yoke) with a vice like grip but it is also essential that your hand doesn't slip off, so gloves that absorb perspiration are useful. They would also protect your hands from fire and injury should you be involved in an accident. Likewise a good set of flying overalls, that fit closely at the neck, ankles and wrists, give some fire protection, should ensure that your clothing doesn't snag controls and will give you zippered or Velcro sealed pockets in which you can keep items essential for the flight safely tucked away where they won't fall out and risk jamming the controls. Footwear should not be so heavy that it deadens your sensitivity to the rudder control but should also afford some measure of protection. Trainers give no real protection against fire or injury; reasonably light leather flying boots do. Many aerobatic aircraft have seats that are designed to take parachutes and, although there is no law or regulation saying you must wear a parachute to do aerobatics, it is good common sense to do so when possible. You are unlikely ever to need a 'chute but you should still make sure you know how to use it. Being stuck in an unrecoverable flat spin, or contending with a structural failure in the air, isn't exactly the best time or place to start working out the technique involved in abandoning the aircraft.

Aerobatics are full of esoteric names. It won't be long before you hear the term Aresti, which comes from the 'Aresti Cryptographic System', a type of shorthand that enables aerobatic manoeuvres to be drawn clearly and simply on paper. An Aresti dictionary contains about 30,000 different aerobatic manoeuvres but before you allow that awesome fact to dissuade you from even starting to learn any of them, take comfort in the knowledge that virtually every one of these is based on just four simple figures. These are the loop, the roll, the stall turn and the spin. How do you get from four to 30,000? Easy; an aeroplane has three planes of movement and if you consider how it is possible to combine and permutate the basic manoeuvres in each of these planes, and in all the intermediate angles that lie between them, you will begin to get the idea.

Types of Manoeuvre

The Inside Loop is probably the easiest manoeuvre for most pilots to perform well and it is also arguably the most spectacular basic manoeuvre for spectators to watch. It consists of a circle flown in the vertical plane with the pilot's head pointing towards the centre of the circle. (A loop was the first intentional aerobatic manoeuvre ever recorded; it was performed by a Russian, Peter Nesterov, on 20 August 1913 at Syretzk near Kiev ... and he was apparently clapped into the guardroom for 'needless audacity' as a reward for his efforts!) The Outside Loop or 'Bunt' has the pilot's head directed towards the outside of the circle and is, in my personal opinion, one of the most pointless and uncomfortable things anyone ever invented to do with an aeroplane. The Slow Roll involves using the ailerons to make the aircraft roll gently around its longitudinal axis, using the rudder and elevators to keep it as near straight and as level as possible. Halfway round you will find yourself hanging on your shoulder straps, so don't forget to pull them tight before you start. Tight straps are a prerequisite for the Stall Turn also. Here the aim is to get the aircraft climbing vertically and then to time your application of rudder exactly correctly, just as the aircraft is pointing vertically into the air and running out of puff towards the top of the climb but before it starts to tailslide backwards. Judge it right and you should achieve a 180° 'cartwheel' after which you have to ease the aircraft out of its subsequent vertical dive. Misjudge it and you can end up with a tailslide, a hammer-head stall, an upward skid and roll, or some other schemozzle. All aircraft have a favourite direction for stall turns. They tend to be easiest to perform to the right in aircraft fitted with British engines such as the Gipsy, Cirrus etc and are best done to the left in those powered by American Lycomings, Continentals etc. The aerobatic spin is not quite the same animal as the one that featured as a compulsory item in the PPL syllabus back in the good old days. Instead, it is a precision manoeuvre in which the pilot times both entry and recovery so as to ensure a predetermined number of turns and in such a way as to exit from the manoeuvre in exactly the desired direction. To achieve this the pilot has to practise until he or she knows the aircraft and its spin performance quite intimately. Perhaps it is the difference between the pilot who is prepared to carry out a whole series of spins one after the other just to get this right, and the pilot to whom more than one spin a week would be anathema, that marks the real difference between a born aerobatic enthusiast and the rest of the pilot population.

All the other aerobatic manoeuvres and sequences are combinations and permutations of these basic four. Some have names with a history. The oldest perhaps is the 'Immelmann Turn'. It is so old that no one is really certain now what manoeuvre it was that Max Franz Immelmann actually flew. The popular belief is that his famous turn was a roll off the top of a loop, but it is doubtful if the Fokker Eindeckers he flew were capable of doing this. It seems more probable that the real Immelmann Turn was a steep climbing turn or what the Americans now term a 'Chandelle' although the truth about what an Immelmann really was is already lost in the mists of aviation antiquity. What is known as a 'Cuban Eight' (a double loop resembling a figure eight on its side) came into being when an American, Len Povey, at that time chief pilot for the Cuban revolutionary Fulgencio Batista, made a mess of a planned manoeuvre at a Miami air display and involuntarily performed this instead. After landing he was asked what that spectacular figure had been, so off the cuff he entitled it 'Cuban Eight'.

During my own days of piloting Gloster Meteors I managed once or twice to execute what was known then as a 'Zurakowski Turn' or 'Zurabatic Cartwheel'. Spectacular to view (and equally so from the pilot's seat) this was named after Gloster's 1950s Polish test pilot Jan Zurakowski, who first performed it in public at Farnborough in 1951. You entered it as if to do a stall turn but when the vertical speed was almost zero and the aircraft was pointing vertically upwards, you chopped the power on one engine, leaving the other at full chat; the aircraft started to perform a normal stall turn but then went right through the vertically down position and up the other side, to complete one and a half rotations in the yawing plane before finally entering a spin. So far as I am aware the Meteor was the only aircraft in which Zurabatic Cartwheels could be performed, although it is said that Zurakowski first managed it in a de Havilland Hornet. From the same era came the 'Porteous Loop' and the 'Derry Turn'. The former name commemorates the way Auster (and Beagle) chief test pilot Ranald Porteus did beautiful flick rolls from the top of a loop while flying an Auster Aiglet, also at Farnborough. (Sadly for the memory of Ranald Porteous, his party trick has now been renamed the Avalanche.) The Derry Turn was a speciality of de Havilland test pilot John Derry and was a positive-g turn initiated by rolling through 270° in the opposite direction. Utterly spectacular, but requiring more rudder power and excess thrust than any PPL is ever likely to have at his or her disposal. Instead you can try your hand (given access to a sufficiently strong and powerful aircraft) at Torque Rolls, Inverted Spins, Hesitation Rolls, Flick Rolls, and Lomcevaks, which are really a whole family of manoeuvres derived from positive or negative flicks, torque reaction and gyroscopic precession. Most of these culminate in the aircraft tumbling end-over-end. Positively not for the novice, nor for the squeamish!

Competitive Sport

Competition aerobatics is a challenging field and one that attracts quite a few dedicated and highly skilled aerobatic pilots. It is recognised as an international sport under the *Fédération Aéronautique Internationale* and its regulations have been drawn up by the International Aerobatics Committee. There are regular aerobatic contests held, not only around the UK, but all around the world. These are pitched at all levels of skill and ability, from club competitions through national contests and up to the International World Aerobatic Championships, which are currently held every two years. In the UK the Royal Aero Club has recognised the British Aerobatic Association (BAeA) as the representative body for the sport. Get involved in the British aerobatic scene and you will probably soon be visiting some of the British Aerobatic Association training camps to learn more of the arts and crafts involved. Then you will soon be able to start participating in competitions with names such as the Kernow, McLean, Don Henry, Roy Legg, McAully, Newbold, Tiger and Air Squadron Trophies. There is seldom a dull period of the year once you get caught up in this demanding and immensely satisfying sport.

Demonstration aerobatics at air shows and other events is something one can aspire to only after long hard hours of dedicated practice, and even then only if you have the aptitude and nerves for it. There is little point in performing a perfect sequence of manoeuvres five thousand feet above the heads of the crowd you are supposed to be entertaining. This is the one case when the otherwise sacrosanct rule about never aerobatting below 3,000 feet above the ground simply has to be ignored. Unfortunately, the statistics concerning the numbers of air show aerobatic pilots who have come to grief whilst performing, only serve to emphasise the importance of that 3,000 feet minimum rule for ordinary mortals. If, despite (or maybe even because of) these statistics, you still have an urge to get into aerobatics at air displays or other public events, you would have first to complete one little formality. It is mandatory for all display pilots to have a Display Authorisation issued by the CAA. So if you have any serious leanings in that direction you had better get hold of CAP 403 on Flying Displays and Special Events and read it up in order to get all the necessary details.

Just for Fun

Luckily however, aerobatics for one's own pleasure and satisfaction, as opposed to competition or display, are something else entirely. Aerobatic flying is something that can be thoroughly enjoyed by most competent pilots after a few hours of suitable training. It has often been said that to be a pilot and never to do aerobatics is rather like being married to a beautiful woman (or to a gorgeous man, presumably) and never to consummate the union. On the other hand (even though the earth is sometimes said to move during it) sexual intercourse seldom seems to cause feelings of vertigo, nausea, air-sickness and vomiting, whilst it has to be admitted that aerobatic flying quite frequently does this to certain pilots. If you happen to be one of these pilots, and if the impulse to throw up still persists after a few lessons, then my advice would simply be to give up at that juncture. There is little point in making yourself miserable whilst trying to do something that should be bringing you pleasure. There are lots of other things you can do with aeroplanes and some of these are bound to suit your particular constitution much better than aerobatics. Swallowing pills or potions is not always a good idea either. Most air-sickness remedies and medicines have the effect of slowing down your reactions and making you sleepy, neither of which side effects is conducive to performing well as a pilot.

Safety Factors

Aerobatic instruction should always start with a revision of stalling and an introduction (if you have never done it before) to spinning and recovery. These are necessary since both form part of aerobatics, often intentionally but occasionally involuntarily, should you happen to make a bit of a mess of a manoeuvre. Then comes recovery from unusual attitudes; you never know when you might find yourself in one of these. Basic instruction in the fundamentals of aerobatics should take somewhere around five or six hours for the average PPL pilot before the instructor is likely to feel ready to let you off on your own to 'slip the surly bonds of Earth and dance the skies on laughter-silvered wings' to use John Magee's words from his poem *High Flight*. Then it is just a matter of practice and, if you want to do it to competition or display standard, still more practice.

Aerobatic flying involves stressing yourself and your aeroplane to a much higher degree than most other forms of flying. This is why you should never be tempted to do aerobatics in an aircraft that is not specifically designed and cleared for the job. It is also why you must be prepared to admit freely if you have done anything in the air that might have overstrained the aircraft or its engine. It is all too easy to pull more g than you intended or to let the engine rpm build up beyond the red line. If you do, and you fail to have the machine carefully inspected afterwards, you could be responsible for a mechanical failure on a subsequent flight; perhaps your own, perhaps someone else's.

Performing aerobatics involves more risk than conventional right way up flying; that much has to be accepted. But the amount of extra risk can be kept within acceptable limits by observing sensible rules. Preflight inspections must be more thorough, including checking that no loose objects are on board, securing all harness straps where they cannot interfere with controls and double-checking harness tightness and buckle locking. HASELL checks are essential before each set of manoeuvres, and the H for height is perhaps the most vital of these; no less than 5,000 feet agl when you start and always stop aerobatics at no lower than 3,000 feet agl. Once a satisfactory aerobatic session is over and you are heading back towards the airfield again, you might quite well find yourself in a slightly euphoric state. You have to make a decided effort then to calm down and try not to behave like those crazy car drivers you can often see on their way home from watching a Grand Prix. Remember you are back in the real world once again, so exercise some restraint and revert to normal airmanship standards as you approach the airfield circuit. Nobody there is really going to appreciate a semi-aerobatic rejoin procedure.

For safety's sake make sure you get a good checkout in the aeroplane involved so you can enjoy your aerobatics without overstraining your aircraft; restrain any impulse you may feel to do aerobatics at low level; exercise your art away from built-up areas and busy airspace and constantly maintain a specially good look out for other aircraft. Your aerobatics should then be pretty safe, as well as being excellent fun. The remainder of your flying in all its aspects should benefit from increased safety too, for there is no other form of flying I know that does quite so much as aerobatics to hone a pilot's skills and to enhance his or her airmanship and self-confidence.

Formation Flying

There is no real reason for me to place this section about Formation Flying immediately after the section about Aerobatics, except that the two seem to be closely associated with each other in the minds of many pilots. This is most probably due to the fact that the quintessence of formation flying often involves those magnificent formation aerobatic displays performed by the Red Arrows, *Frecce Tricolori* and *Patrouille de France* military teams, and by the Rothmans, Toyota and other (generally company sponsored) civilian formation teams which perform at many air shows. This type of spectacular formation flying is certainly beyond the capabilities of most private pilots; the many hours of flying that are involved in perfecting the performance of a team like the Red Arrows would cost far more than most civilian pilots could ever afford. Yet there is no reason at all why you should not learn at least some of the basics of formation flying.

What use is formation flying? Like aerobatics, its practical uses in civil flying are limited but it does help tremendously to develop your general handling skills, reactions and powers of anticipation. It can occasionally also be of practical value. Being able to follow a shepherd aircraft if you ever were to become lost, possibly above cloud, is one example of where the ability to formate safely could be very useful. Another would be if your airspeed indicator failed for any reason; it could then be an enormous help in maintaining accurate approach and landing speeds if you were able to formate on another aircraft of similar performance; better by far than stalling as you tried to turn finals. If you are ever called upon to assist in checking the operation of another aircraft's undercarriage it is a great help when you are confident about flying in formation with it. Sometimes it can also be handy to be able to fly a non-radio aircraft in formation with a radio equipped one in order to let it use the other's radio calls to gain entry to restricted airspace. Air-to-air photography can be a hazardous business if the pilots involved have no experience of formation flying, but it becomes much easier if the pilot of at least one of the aircraft is skilled in the art of keeping station.

For certain species of birds, of course, formation flying has been part of their airborne repertoire since time immemorial. Geese, ducks and swans are well known exponents of the art but no ornithologist seems to be absolutely certain why they do it. Theories abound, concerning self-protection, migratory navigation and the possibility that weaker or more fatigued birds at the rear gain some extra lift from vortices left behind by the leaders. For military pilots too, formation flying has long been a basic part of flying. WW1 pilots of the Royal Flying Corps (and their French and German counterparts) soon learned to keep one another company in the air to generate additional fire-power, to have extra pairs of eyes watching for the enemy and to give each other mutual support. No-one who saw them will ever forget the sight and the sound of the vast formations of US bombers and their escort fighters in WW2, as they formed up over England and resolutely flew in unbroken formation across enemy territory to their targets. The majority of the world's military pilots are still trained to fly in close formation and are kept in regular practice at it.

If you fancy the idea of flying in close proximity to another aeroplane then you must learn how to do it properly. Just like aerobatics, formation flying is not something you should try to teach yourself. Get hold of an instructor to show you how. That might be something of a problem in itself, for it is not by any means every instructor who is able to fly formation, never mind teach others how to do it. In UK flying circles, if you look for an instructor who occasionally is seen wearing an RAF or RN tie then you might strike lucky. But for safety's sake resist any temptation to have a go at formation flying without being taught the basics first. I have seen ad hoc attempts at formation flying made by private pilots to impress friends on the ground. Believe me, they wouldn't impress anyone. And I have also lost a good friend as a result of an attempted formation air-to-air photographic session where a misunderstanding brought one of the aircraft to grief, killing all on board. It takes quite a lot of skill and practice to fly safely in close proximity to other aircraft and to follow your formation leader. The exercise is particularly demanding if the air is at all turbulent or if the aircraft are not of similar types or at least of similar performance.

Formation Protocol

Conventionally, aircraft in a formation are numbered; the leader is always number 1 and when flying in a symmetrical formation those aircraft to the leader's left usually have odd numbers and those to the right, even. (This system is the RAF one; if your instructor happens to have been taught formation flying in the Fleet Air Arm then you may well be taught the RN system which is, of course, different.) There are several standard formations and dozens of elaborate ones such as Concorde and others flown by the Red Arrows etc. The simplest is probably the Vic formation, where each of the following aircraft try to station themselves in a Vee shape, their wingtips level with the tailplane of the aircraft ahead and about half a span out from the wingtip. In Line Abreast, the wing aircraft move forward to align their wingtips with the leader's wingtips. Echelon Port is like Vic but with all aircraft to the leader's left and stepped towards the rear. Echelon Starboard is the other way round (these are also now known as Echelon Left and Echelon Right). In Line Astern the leader is straight ahead of, but above, the next aircraft and any subsequent aircraft are similarly stepped down so that they avoid flying in the slipstream of preceding machines. The last of the standard formations needs at least four aircraft and is the Box, which is a simple Vic with number 4 stepped down and directly behind the leader, wingtips aligned with the tailplane of numbers 2 and 3. It is useful to spend some time on the ground looking carefully at the aircraft you are going to be flying alongside, picking out how you are going to align yourself with it, getting familiar with what its perspective looks like when your wingtip is roughly half a span off its wingtip.

There are other conventions you might have to learn too, such as conventional signs that are always used by the leader in open cockpit aircraft (and often in closed cockpit aircraft too) to indicate the next intended manoeuvres and conventional radio calls that are used for the same purpose. These calls take the form of 'Manoeuvre, manoeuvre, GO!' with GO being the signal to start the 'Turning right' or 'Smoke on' or whatever. A thorough briefing before flight is essential so that all pilots involved know in advance what is the aim of the trip, what action is proposed in the event of bad weather, where the formation will meet to join up (always an interesting stage that, for the newcomer to formation flying) and what changes of formation are anticipated during the flight. In the initial stages, formation take-off and landing is a strict no-no, and even for experienced pilots, ATC agreement for this must be obtained in advance. The easiest way of joining formation is usually to approach the leader from behind and below, adjusting power as you gradually slip into the desired position; this avoids rushing along level at full throttle to catch up and then finding yourself unable to slow down soon enough to avoid overtaking number 1. That can be distinctly dangerous if you lose sight of the lead ship behind you, as well as being just ever so slightly embarrassing.

Once you have mastered station keeping while straight and level, gentle climbs and descents should present you with no great problems. Turning comes next; gentle ones only, 15° bank angle at most to start with. The aircraft on the outside of a turn have farther to fly than the lead ship, so need a bit of extra throttle to keep up. Conversely the inside aircraft have to slow down a bit. Changing from one formation to another looks childishly simple when you see the expert formation teams doing it. When you try it yourself you will soon find that it is quite an art form and one that you need to rehearse on the ground before you ever attempt it in the air. The trick of course is to make absolutely certain that no two aeroplanes ever try to occupy the same bit of the sky during the change.

Being close to other aircraft in the air is something you normally avoid, for obvious safety reasons. When you deliberately set out to keep close company with other aircraft you are, of course, making your flying that little bit more hazardous, but the extra risk is not great provided you all stick to the rules. Never attempt any DIY impromptu formation; that is simply asking for trouble. Always prepare thoroughly for the trip and ensure that all the pilots concerned really do know what is going to be performed. All you have to do is treat formation flying with the respect it deserves and you will find it will become yet another exciting and satisfying facet of your flying.

Splashdown

Seaplane flying is something which most British pilots associate in their minds more with Canada, New Zealand or Florida perhaps, than with the UK. Yet the opportunity exists at more than one location in the UK, to learn how to fly from water. This can be an interesting experience and one that is decidedly different from the way the vast majority of flyers get their aeroplanes into the air and back down again. It must be admitted that a seaplane rating is of but limited practical use in Britain. There are very few amphibians and seaplanes on the British register and fewer still that are available for hire. Although a number of individuals have tried to expand the opportunities for water based flying in this country, suitable facilities still remain few and far between. There are certain legal complications, associated with the law of trespass, which can adversely affect the operation of aircraft from water in England, but in Scotland the law of trespass is entirely different (virtually non-existent in point of fact) and it is permissible to operate a seaplane from almost any loch or other body of water in Scotland. This is one good reason why Britain's busiest water flying centre, Caledonian Seaplanes, which offers you the opportunity of adding a seaplane rating to your PPL in magnificent surroundings, is located at Lochearnhead in Perthshire.

Alternatively, float plane instruction is available in various other places in the world including (close to both Disney World and Orlando in Florida) Jack Brown's Seaplane Base in Winter Haven. This centre claims to have trained more seaplane pilots than any other facility in the world. It is a long way to travel if the seaplane rating is all you are after and the relatively small difference in aircraft hourly hire rates between the Scottish and the American establishments will scarcely cover the travel costs involved. The seaplane rating should involve an average PPL pilot in little more than five hours of flying and can easily be completed within a couple of days. The UK rating also involves passing a 20 question multiple-choice exam paper on seamanship set by the CAA, who also publish a guide to studying for the seamanship examination. Another useful bible for the would-be water flyer is *How to Fly Floats* published by Edo Corporation, the well known American manufacturer of seaplane floats. You should really read both these publications, and be sure you have thoroughly digested their contents, before you start the airborne and waterborne parts of the seaplane rating course.

The airborne part is really quite insignificant. If you can fly a land-plane, particularly if you have some experience of tailwheel aircraft, then you can fly a float plane. The weight of the floats reduces climb performance a little compared to a similar wheeled machine and you need to apply rather bigger bootfulls of rudder to compensate for the machine's altered directional stability. The aircraft also stalls at a slightly higher speed and when the throttle is closed (or if the engine fails on take-off) the drag of the floats makes the nose drop quite sharply, the airspeed falls rapidly away and the glide approach is appreciably steeper than normal. But it is essentially the business of handling the float plane on the surface of water that you have to learn; that and getting the beast off the water and back on to it again. A bit of experience in dinghy sailing helps here, to give you some idea of how you should handle the movement of the aircraft on the water, counteract wind effect and steer to where you intend to start the take-off run. With wide expanses of water normally available, take-off and landing can usually be into wind, so crosswind effects can be forgotten. There are lots of strange new terms for you to learn too. You will find out how to 'sail' (or 'idle taxi') the aircraft slowly, 'displace' (or 'taxi') it slightly faster, 'plough' (or in America 'plow') it fast enough to lift the front of the floats up clear of the water, or 'step-taxi' it, when the floats are skimming the surface at perhaps 30 knots or so. After step-taxying is the actual take-off and on a low power training float plane it sometimes seems to take an eternity to reach this stage. If the water is glassy smooth your little floatplane may in fact never reach unstick speed at all, unless you use one of the tricks of the marine flyer's trade.

From Airborne to Waterborne

Water landings, nearly always being into wind, present few problems, unless the water happens to be glassy smooth. It can then be infernally difficult to judge your height above the surface. Bear in mind that the floats are rigidly attached to the aircraft with no oleos or bungees or leaf-spring undercarriage legs to help absorb any jolts. It is obvious that hefty impacts with the water surface are to be avoided, otherwise damage to the airframe is quite liable to occur. To achieve a gentle touchdown in smooth water conditions, you sometimes have to make a low pass and chuck out something that floats to give you a clue as to where the surface level is as you make your next approach to touch down. Otherwise you can try to touch down close to something like a buoy, a shrub on the water's edge or a moored boat, which has the same effect. Or you just have to descend very gradually, holding the airspeed just a knot or five above the stall, and wait patiently for the float keels to score the surface. At that juncture you close the throttle and hold the stick back and you should be safely down. My most vivid memory of my own limited experience of water flying, is of watching the opposite shore of the loch as it seemed to be approaching me with undesirable rapidity and my becoming supremely conscious of the fact that manufacturers always forget to fit seaplanes with any brakes! Fortunately, once a seaplane decelerates a little with the stick held well back, it comes 'off the step' and slows up quite smartly. That is the time you stop being an aircraft pilot and find yourself back in charge of the equivalent of an aerial catamaran.

Getting your seaplane rating is one thing, using it is another. Opportunities for that are somewhat limited in Britain and you may be pushed even to keep it valid with the necessary one seaplane flight each year. None the less a seaplane rating isn't something that many people acquire and it is definitely a nice piece of one-upmanship to have, another feather in your flyer's cap. As something to talk about around the flying club bar of an evening it will cap your clubmates' tales of IMC ratings any day. It is not expensive, as flying accomplishments go, and it lets you extend your piloting experience in yet another interesting and stimulating direction.

Rallies, Fly-ins and other Fun Events

There is no need for you to become a member of anything other than the world of private flying before you can take part in and enjoy many of the dozens of open events organised every year by enthusiasts all over the country, and indeed all over the world. I am thinking about all those happenings that go under the various names of Fly-In, Air Rally, Breakfast Patrol, Wings and Wheels, Easter Air Weekend, Old-Timer Meeting and so on. Thumb through your favourite flying magazine and see what is on offer and which of the events you feel might be of most interest to you. Once you have made the slight initial effort of 'phoning the organisers to put your name down for the fly-in (or whatever they call it) you begin to get sucked into the mainstream of things. You do a bit of flight planning to get to wherever the get-together is taking place and then, when the great day arrives and you have actually flown in, you will perhaps start to wonder why on earth you bothered to go there at all. Everyone there, apart from yourself, will seem to know everyone else and you will quite probably, at the beginning, feel somewhat left out of things. But flying enthusiasts being what they are, you can be pretty sure that it will not be long before you are every bit as caught up in things as all the old hands. You are highly unlikely to reach the end of the event without making solemn promises to be back again next year, or to meet some of the others at another happening which is due to take place in the interim. Many of these events involve some degree of usually fairly light-hearted competition. Hardy annual events of this type which are popular with British pilots include the International Air Rallies of Jersey, Guernsey and Malta, the Granite City Air Rally in Aberdeen and the Kilkenny International Rally. It is quite possible to attend and enjoy these without bothering to participate in their competitive aspects if these tend to be at all off-putting from your point of view. Then there are the many fly-ins, under various names and guises, which are essentially social in nature but sometimes do have a little of the competitive element included, just to spice them up a bit. Again these are always voluntary. You won't be pressured into making spot landings, or dropping flour bags, or flying in aerial treasure hunts, if you would rather just quietly enjoy the sunshine and the company. Having attended many of these gatherings, I'll be surprised if you don't soon find yourself itching to have a go at some of the less serious of these little adventures. It all adds to the fun of what generally turns out to be a thoroughly enjoyable day or weekend out.

Set your own World Record

Mention world records to most PPL pilots and they will immediately think of pioneering pilots like Bert Hinckler, Amy Johnson and Charles Lindbergh, or more modern aviation achievers such as Dick Rutan and Jeana Yeager flying un-refuelled and non-stop around the world in their Voyager aircraft. Alternatively their minds will turn immediately to powerful jet aircraft like the Lockheed Blackbird which has hurtled from London to New York at an average speed of just under 1250 knots (2,320 kilometres per hour, to be precise). Then there is the altitude record for winged aircraft which is now well above 350,000 feet (106,680 m). There is precious little chance surely, of any pilot of a typical light aircraft getting a look in here.

Surprisingly enough, there is. If you are interested, and have at least 100 hours P1 time in your logbook, there is no reason at all why you shouldn't take a crack at having your name added to the list of illustrious world record holders which is kept by the *Fédération Aéronautique Internationale* (FAI) in Paris. There isn't even any need for you to go to the trouble of contacting the FAI. They have a representative in the UK in the form of the Royal Aero Club and it is the RAeC's Records, Racing and Rally Association, which looks after all record attempts by British registered fixed-wing powered aircraft, and by all UK pilots. There is no need either, strangely enough, to fly a particularly fast, powerful or long-range aircraft in order to be able to set a world record. Still interested? Or simply puzzled, the way most pilots are when they first find out about this record breaking business?

There are literally thousands of records within the flying scene that have either never yet been set, or have already been made and are therefore already on the FAI's record books just waiting for someone else to come along and break them. In many cases that someone else could easily be a 101 hour PPL pilot flying a perfectly standard training or touring light aircraft. The business of setting and breaking records need not even be a very expensive exercise for you, provided you are sensible and choosy about the record or records you want to set or break. The easiest to tackle are the speed records from one point to another. Endurance records and distance records are a bit trickier for normal light aircraft to establish these days and altitude records involve some special equipment, including a barograph. If you were silly enough to try something obvious for your speed record, like London to Paris, you will immediately run into problems for lots of expensive hardware has already pushed that one (and many others like it) well out of reach of the private pilot in a standard Cessna trainer. There is, though, no need for record attempts to be made between major or obvious city pairs. You might well find that Cambridge to Cork, Norwich to Namur, or perhaps Plymouth to Poitiers, are routes all waiting for records to be set in your class of aircraft. Yes, even if someone has already chalked up their name on the record for a particular route while flying one type of aircraft, that doesn't mean you cannot set up a record of your own for the same route while flying a larger or smaller aircraft. There are categories for land-planes, seaplanes and amphibians and different divisions for piston engines, turboprops, jet engines and even rocket powered aircraft. The piston engine land plane category is further subdivided into six weight defined classes, with take-off weights under 300 kg, 500 kg, 1,000 kg, 1,750 kg, 3,000 kg and 6,000 kg. As you can imagine this gives plenty of scope for all sorts of aircraft to set all sorts of speed records.

To go about setting a record (and incidentally, if successful, acquiring a handsome Record Certificate to frame and hang on the office or living-room wall) you must first get a Royal Aero Club Competitor's Licence, which will cost you just £30. Apply for this to the RAeC, Records, Racing and Rally Association. Once you have this (and be warned, the application form asks you to find someone willing to sign certifying that he or she confirms you are sane!) you are free to decide which world record to attempt. The RAeC will check for you whether any route you propose is available for a new record, or if you have an existing record to beat. Perhaps the next holiday trip you are planning (or your next business flight to see a customer or visit an exhibition) might be an opportunity for you to set or break a world air speed record as well?

There is another fee to pay before you go, in order to register the attempt in advance with the Royal Aero Club but from there on the formalities are few. The RAeC doesn't tie you down too closely so far as the time or the date of the attempt are concerned, knowing that weather is an important factor. Nor is it necessary for you to have RAeC observers to check you out at take-off and in at your destination. The times of take-off and landing, as recorded by Air Traffic Control at a controlled airfield, are readily accepted. If the attempt is between points other than controlled airfields, then it gets a little trickier, but the RAeC might even go so far as to have an official observer fly with you in the aircraft to confirm timings.

Some private pilots have become quite hooked on setting world records. Most others are quite content to have just one or two of the record certificates to impress their friends and colleagues. Record setting is certainly not a complicated pastime, nor is it necessarily expensive. Sometimes it might even be possible to find commercial sponsorship for a world record attempt if you use your imagination in picking the record and go about things the correct way, making use of any contacts you have. Record breaking sounds quite an exciting affair, yet it doesn't add any extra risk or danger to the flying involved and the aircraft insurance policy will normally cover an attempt of the type outlined here without any extra premium. Adding a record attempt to almost any international flight can give the trip an interesting bit of extra kick. (Records can be set within one country too, but there is a minimum distance then of at least 400 km, which is approximately 216 nm.) Selecting, planning and carrying out an occasional world air record attempt can be great fun and gives any PPL another good reason to use his or her licence in yet another imaginative way.

The Dawn to Dusk

This is another event in which you might like to consider participating, and which again doesn't require you to become a member of any special organisation. The Dawn to Dusk International Flying Competition is an annual competition in which private pilots are invited to stretch their imaginations and broaden their flying experience. Sponsored by Pooley's (of *Flight Guide* and *Aeroshopping* fame) this is an original and unusual sort of contest in which you, the entrant, can write most of the rules yourself. You decide what sort of flying you might like to do and to what purpose, then make your own plans, set your own time (within fairly broad limits) and off you go and do it. Despite the name (which isn't really taken too literally) it is certainly not necessary for you to stay in the air from first light until sunset. There is, however, an airborne minimum time of eight hours to be observed (or seven if you have logged under 100 hours as P1). You are at liberty to spend your Dawn to Dusk day doing something you have dreamed up all by yourself, based on your own interests and initiative. You may consider your flight to be educational, historical, geographical or inspirational, or you may decide to fly some other mission of the 'just because it is there' sort. The main requirement is that whatever you endeavour to do it must have a fair degree of originality to it. Having flown your competition flight, all that remains for you to do is to write up your log and flight description and send these off, together with all your maps and charts, landing and fuel receipts etc. These make up your entry. Then you just have to await the judges verdict on what you have submitted to them.

The Dawn to Dusk International Flying Competition can be flown by any pilot, using any type of aircraft from a microlight upwards. The simpler the aircraft, the more marks are awarded for any particular task, to take into consideration the extra effort involved. Low hours pilots also score more marks for similar tasks than more experienced contenders. The marking is rather a complicated matter but in the end the winner receives the premier award of the Duke of Edinburgh Trophy. According to the Duke of Edinburgh himself (who has for many years taken a keen interest in the Competition) he suspects that the marking is there just to give the judges something to do; the real satisfaction comes from taking part. The Dawn to Dusk certainly has inspired some interesting and challenging flying in the past and often proves to be the ideal catalyst to get some private pilots out of their comfortable, but boring, ruts to discover for themselves just how much more challenge and satisfaction the flying of small aeroplanes has to offer.

Air Racing

During the interwar years air races were one of the mainstays of light aviation. Enthusiastic pilots, professional and amateur alike, turned up to race each other in such events as the King's Cup Air Race, which was first held in 1922 over a course from Croydon to Glasgow and back. The Schneider Trophy dates back even earlier, to its debut in Monaco in 1913. The Grosvenor Challenge Cup was for aircraft of 150hp or less. There have been many 'one-off' air races like the MacRobertson Race of 1934 from England to Australia or the *Daily Mail's* Transatlantic Race of 1969. Now, however, these spectacles seem to have lost a great deal of their appeal to the public and air races tend to be the preserve of a limited number of keen pilots, enthusiasts and specialists. You can still enter for and fly a Schneider Trophy race, but it bears little resemblance to the enormously prestigious events of that name that were held in the 1930s. On the other hand, the average PPL pilot had no chance of participating in these, whilst the current Schneider Trophy Races most definitely are open to all, as long as they qualify. Other events of this nature which make up the air racing calendar in the British Isles include the City Livery Trophy, Bill Entress Trophy, Battle of Britain Trophy, Claddagh Trophy, Grosvenor Trophy, Stewards Cup and the King's Cup Races. So if you develop a taste for air racing and want to compete against the best, there are plenty of events to choose from at venues all around the UK and Ireland. There is a racing pilots' championship, and points towards winning this can be earned by securing a place in each of the qualifying events.

Most of these races are based on the handicap system and so to some extent you are racing the handicapper as much as the other competitors. The handicaps are calculated on the known performance of the aircraft involved, and the handicapper's aim is to have each aircraft take off at a given time dependent on these calculations, so that theoretically all should arrive simultaneously at the finish. The fact that they don't is due to how well the aeroplanes have been tweaked to squeeze extra performance out of them, to the flying skills of the pilots and to a certain measure of good or bad luck. You can enter most of these races in almost any type of aircraft: homebuilts, old-timers, production Pipers and Cessnas etc, and occasionally you even find the odd piston engine or jet fighter entered. The air racing scene is no place for owners or pilots who dislike the idea of their aero-engines being belted at full throttle virtually throughout each race, nor for those who are uncomfortable with the idea of hurtling round pylons or markers at low level and overtaking slower aircraft which loom up in front of you during the race. Overtaking is easier than on a Formula 1 Grand Prix motor racing circuit, but it can still have its exciting moments.

Excitement Unlimited

For real excitement, especially from the spectator point of view, what is known as Unlimited Class air racing is hard to beat. The home for this is in America, more specifically at Reno in Nevada, where each September the National Air Races are held. The aircraft are nearly all World War II piston engine fighters, which scream along at low level over the desert, throttles wide open, racing at up to 400 mph around circuits marked by tall pylons at each corner. There are also many other races in America for all sorts of aircraft types. What they call the T-6 Races are restricted to what we know in Britain as the North American Harvard two-seat trainer. Then there are Formula One races for small, fixed undercarriage aircraft with limited engine displacement; these are also raced occasionally in Britain, with Duxford a popular venue for the European Formula One Championships.

Like aerobatics, air racing is not every pilot's cup of tea but it does tend to become a real fascination for many pilots who decide to give it a try. Competing in the typical races run in the British Isles you will find is not an over expensive activity for an enthusiastic pilot to pursue. Unless your pockets are very deep and well lined I would strongly advise you to steer clear of Unlimited Class racing though. That is horrendously expensive stuff. Even as a spectator on the ground, watching the gaggle of different types of aircraft inexorably catching up with each other as they approach the finish of a handicap air race, can make a thrilling spectacle. Imagine what it could do for your blood pressure if you were actually up there piloting one of the average speed aircraft, trying all the tricks you knew in order to overhaul the slower types ahead of you and wondering all the while whether there was some faster machine breathing down your neck and liable to pip you at the post. If that sort of idea gets your adrenalin pumping and your pulse racing, maybe you should think about getting your aeroplane racing too.

Precision Flying

Do you enjoy meticulous airmanship, skilful piloting and really accurate navigation? If your answer is yes, then you might be interested in the British Precision Pilots' Association. They organise competitions and events several times a year and these quite often include a beginners' introductory event, where you can find out more details of what precision flying is all about before you commit yourself in any way. After your introduction you are permitted one full competitive event as an outsider and then, if you wish to continue with the sport, you must join the Association. You can't really ask for a much fairer way than that of introducing you gently to the sport. Although it is still very much a minority sport among British pilots, precision flying is very popular in other parts of the world, notably Eastern Europe and South America, and there are regular international competitions which culminate in the biannual World Championships.

Precision Flying has long been a very important part of the training of military and naval pilots but the idea of civilian precision flying competitions appears to have originated during the late 1940s in Sweden. The early contests that were held in Sweden were designed simply as fun ways of encouraging private pilots to polish up the basic skills they had learned during their PPL course. Basic among these skills was visual navigation, with the emphasis on the chart and compass, stopwatch and the famous Eyeball Mark I. These skills are still the key elements of most precision flying competitions. Entrants are expected to do different things at different competitions (it would after all soon become a bit boring otherwise) and to some extent the navigation exercises can be said to resemble orienteering routes or car club rally and treasure hunt events. The organisers pit their wits against the competitors, who in turn put their skills to work against each other. A typical competition could perhaps involve you being given somewhat cryptic route instructions, from which you have to prepare a flight plan within a given time limit and without the aid of any electronic whizz-sticks, Psion organisers etc. You then have to fly the route you have worked out and carry out a series of exercises during the flight. These could include pinpointing photographs of ground features near the track (and perhaps being sharp enough to identify some photos you've been given that are of things that resemble, but aren't really the ones you are actually flying over). Or you could have to mark your charts to indicate precisely where conspicuous 'targets' have been laid out, or describe what colour or shape these targets are. To make life more interesting you are also being timed by ground observers at turning points and elsewhere, and you are expected to pass each checkpoint within a very narrow margin (+/- a couple of seconds or so) of the ETAs calculated from the aircraft's declared airspeed. Fastest aircraft generally are flagged off first, slowest last, to prevent bunching or overtaking en route.

At the end of this navex there is often something along the lines of a spot landing contest, but this is generally rather more sophisticated than your average club affair. You could be asked to make one landing in a normal configuration with power and flaps as required, then a flapless glide approach to land or (if the organisers were feeling particularly evil minded that day) maybe a glide approach that has to clear a two-metre high obstruction just 50 metres from the touchdown marker line. You don't just lose points for over or undershooting the line; they mark you down for landing nose-wheel first or together with the mains, for bouncing, touching one main wheel before the other, etc. After all, it *is* called precision flying! At some of the bigger competitions, instead of having eagle-eyed watchers to determine where your touchdown actually happens, the runway has a special carpet spread over it at the critical area. Pressure cells embedded in this mat are then used to give a technologically accurate definition of your precise landing point. It is very difficult to argue about these results afterwards.

No Need for Special Gear
One great advantage that this sport has is that you do not need to kit up with lots of expensive special equipment or even a special aeroplane. Slow aircraft have certain advantages over fast ships, the better ground visibility from high wing machines gives them a slight advantage over their low wing brethren. Polish precision pilots love the Wilga with its superb visibility, lots of cockpit glazing, high wing and excellent slow speed performance. But plenty of British pilots swear by bog-standard Cessna 152s or 172s and the like. Some real fanatics have fitted their aircraft with little extra downward looking windows that can help then spot ground landmarks and targets. Some like to remove the right-hand front seat to give the pilot more elbow-room and the rear seat navigator more space for his or her clobber. And that inexpensive clobber, charts, maps, stopwatches, marker pens, pencils, erasers and clipboard, really comprise the only accoutrements you need before you can participate.

Essentials for Success
Precision flying always requires very thorough preflight preparation, really accurate piloting and navigation skills, and sharp eyes. Frequently you need a twisted mind to work out some of the cryptic

clues and invariably you must have the patience and ability to forgive each other after landing, for all the 'stupid so-and-so' epithets you probably used during the competition. Just like a good hectic car rally in fact. It can be great fun and local (as opposed to international) events are usually pretty informal, although even at these you will find most of the entrants take the whole thing reasonably seriously. Have a go at a precision flying competition sometime. It is likely to mean that next time you are heading off to navigate yourself from A to B, you will probably do it a great deal more accurately. And, as another bonus, you could well find yourself making a far better landing than usual when you reach B too.

Join the Club

This chapter does not by any means contain a complete listing of all the specialist activities that are ready and waiting to welcome any private pilot who wants to come on in and join the fun. As well as the various well known flying clubs and schools, flying groups and aircraft partnerships, there are many other organisations and associations that can help broaden a private pilot's interests and enhance his or her overall enjoyment of flying.

World's Biggest Pilots' Club

Becoming a member of the Aircraft Owners and Pilots Association of the UK (AOPA UK), which forms part of the largest pilot organisation in the world, International AOPA, does make you feel more an integral part of the private flying movement in this country, and your membership also helps give private flying a useful and authoritative voice to argue its own case. Most European countries, and many other states worldwide, have their own AOPAs, all of which are affiliated to the international body IAOPA, the membership of which totals well over 400,000 pilots. As a member of AOPA UK you get its magazine, *Light Aviation* and you will also receive newsletters that help keep you up to date with what is happening within the British private flying scene. It offers members a legal first-aid service for any aviation related problem. You can also, as a member, apply for an 'Aircrew Card'. This identifies you as a pilot and can be used to get discounts at various hotels and other places. AOPA UK also has links with car hire companies that offer members special rates, insurance companies (aviation, car, house and life) and finance companies. Overall AOPA endeavours to make flying more useful, safer, less expensive and more fun.

Becoming an International Partner Member of the American parent organisation gives you access to AOPA's Internet (Compuserve-based) database of aviation information and several other privileges. Unfortunately most of these privileges are largely irrelevant unless you are flying within the United States. Other national AOPAs also have their own membership privileges.

True to Type

Owners' clubs or Type clubs are certainly useful organisations to belong to if you are an aircraft owner, and they can frequently be helpful even if you just habitually fly the same type of aircraft. Many of these clubs publish regular newsletters that keep you in the picture concerning new developments, snags that may have been encountered by other pilots, solutions for some of these snags, maintenance tips and so on. These clubs often organise meetings or fly-ins too and these can offer wonderful opportunities to meet people with interests (in the aviation field at least) which are similar to your own. Flying in to attend these meetings (many of which are held in conjunction with similar clubs in other European countries) is also an excellent way of encouraging yourself to do something different and possibly a little more adventurous than is your usual wont with your aeroplane. Active groups of this nature have been formed in Britain around many types of aircraft, including vintage Pipers, Aeroncas, the AA/Grumman/Gulfstream range, Robins and others.

Home for Home-builders

The largest fly-in event in Europe each year is the one organised by the Popular Flying Association, the PFA Rally. The PFA is the backbone of all the home-building activity that goes on in this country and if you decide, after reading Chapter 8, that you want to make a move into aircraft ownership via that route, then you will certainly become a member of PFA. This does not by any means imply that other pilots who fly factory built aircraft are not also welcome as members. Quite the contrary. Membership of the PFA is another way of learning a great deal about your hobby of light aircraft flying, from what may, to you, be a fresh and fascinating angle. If you are harbouring any dark thoughts at the back of your mind about spending all your spare time out in the garage or garden shed with saws and tinsnips and pliers, or plastic, adhesives and glasspaper, you owe it to yourself to become a PFA member. That should sort things out for you one way or another. You may begin to marvel at the longsuffering dedication of these crazy plane-building people (and their even longer suffering partners) and go off the whole idea. It is far better to do this, if you are going to, before you have committed yourself too far technically or financially to the project. On the other hand you may well find yourself gradually becoming unable to resist the idea of weekends and long evenings of creative craftsmanship, after your normal work is over; seemingly endless hours of wood and metalwork, gluing, painting and polishing. Long hours certainly, but hours which do eventually culminate in the ineffable satisfaction of taking to the air in something that you have created with your own two hands.

All around the country there are branches of the PFA (called 'Struts') at which local members get together to discuss the relative merits of different home-built designs, share experiences, make contact with the engineers and inspectors who oversee all building projects, and generally enjoy each others' company. I've come across some enthusiasts who actually join the PFA and build their own aircraft, even before they bothered to qualify for a PPL, and I have enjoyed being a member of the PFA for many years, without ever having had the courage to start building anything more enterprising than a model aircraft. PFA has space for, and welcomes, all types of flyers. This fact will immediately become apparent to you should you ever decide to join them in their annual pilgrimage to that great aviation event, the PFA Rally.

Association for Woman Pilots

There is another British pilots' association which will be of interest only to what is regrettably a small proportion of the pilots who are likely to read this book. It is also the only pilots' association in the UK whose membership is gender limited. I am referring here to the British Women Pilots' Association (BWPA). One of the aims of the BWPA is to turn flying into less of a minority interest activity for women, and another is to do all they can to remove the so-called 'glass ceiling' which tends to limit career prospects for female pilots. Since it is not one of the aims of this book to deal in any detail with commercial flying matters, I shall not pursue that second objective any farther here. It is worth pointing out, however, that many women who are private pilots, and whose aim is to continue flying for pleasure rather than to make a career in aviation, do find membership of the BWPA both useful and interesting. There are local branches in various parts of the country and the BWPA is a great help in bringing women pilots together to discuss their common interests.

Agricultural Aviation and Aerodrome Ownership

If you happen to be engaged in agriculture, and particularly if you regularly fly to and from farm strips rather than international airports, then you could well find that the Flying Farmers' Association (FFA) would be an organisation of considerable interest to you. One of its main functions is to assist FFA members in the exchange of ideas, problems and solutions on all manner of themes that affect farm flying. These can include subjects ranging from planning permits to petrol pumps, set-aside to strip mowing, noise abatement to uninvited visitors. Again this is very much a minority interest Association, but as such it can and does offer its members a good specialised service that is difficult for them to obtain from anywhere else. Similarly, the Aerodrome Owners' Association is not one that will be of interest to more than a few of the private pilots who read this volume, but for those who happen to be involved in the ownership or operation of an aerodrome, the AOA offers a wealth of shared knowledge and experience that could well turn out to be of inestimable value.

Chapter 7

Pilots' Playthings

Hand-held Radios

In Chapter 2, whilst we were considering how some pilots have to over-come a little diffidence before they feel comfortable about making proper use of the aircraft radio, mention was made of the wide range of portable aircraft band VHF receivers that are on the market. These can be very useful for listening in to aircraft transmissions and familiarising yourself with radiotelephony procedures but they are a different breed of radio entirely from the hand-held radios being discussed here. More properly known as transceivers, these are combined VHF receivers and transmitters. They normally have a frequency range that spans the entire aircraft VHF band, from 118.000 MHz to 137.000 MHz. Frequently a navigation facility is built in which permits use of the unit as a VOR receiver, complete with a Course Deviation Indicator (CDI) display on the unit's LCD screen.

These transceivers have two main uses. Pilots of microlights and many home-built aircraft use them as their main VHF radio for all normal radiotelephony (RT) in their aircraft. Other pilots who fly aircraft equipped with one or more panel mounted VHF radios, also carry hand-held transceivers with them in their pilot cases, mainly as emergency back-up in case of failure of the built-in aircraft sets. It is not all that unusual for a panel mounted VHF radio to become unusable for one reason or another. I have known the aircraft's alter-nator to fail and once all the remaining on-board electrical power from the battery has drained away, the radios are entirely useless. Occasionally the failure of a relay, or the sticking of a microphone button, is enough to put a built-in VHF set out of action. Even a defec-tive frequency selector can leave a pilot unable to change to the channel required at the time. If any such misfortune strikes while you are flying, you can be very glad indeed of a hand-held radio if there is one with you in the cockpit. These sets are also of potentially life-saving value in the event of a ditching (or even a forced landing in desolate country)

139

when a hand-held transceiver can provide a vital channel of communication with rescue services.

Their power can come from a cigar lighter socket or from a battery pack. This can be of the rechargeable variety, or if the unit is to be used solely as an emergency stand-by, then an alkaline battery is probably better, since it holds its charge for a much longer period than a rechargeable. Since a hand-held has lots of other valuable potential uses though, I feel it would be a pity if you were to keep yours only for use in emergencies. It frequently comes in handy on the ground, not just to eavesdrop on airline pilot chatter but (if you are in a favoured area) to get Volmet broadcast weather information. At busy airfields where start-up clearance is required, you can use your hand-held transceiver for this purpose to save the drain on the aircraft batteries. (These have to supply not just the VHF radio as soon as you switch the master switch on, but also the gyros etc.) Waiting for the previous pilot to return with the club or group aircraft, you can get on with something else useful whilst keeping half an ear open for the 'rejoining' call to come through on the hand-held, instead of simply sitting aimlessly waiting for the aircraft to turn up.

Restricted Range

The performance of hand-held sets in the air has become much more effective since the early models first appeared but they still have their limitations. Their range is limited by their output transmission power to a maximum radius of approximately 30 miles. Even that is not attainable unless the batteries are well charged and the aircraft is fairly high; from around 1,500 feet you are lucky if you can contact a ground station any farther off than about fifteen miles. You can however usually receive ground transmissions (and aircraft transmissions too) from much farther away than that. The VOR facility works best when the antenna of the hand-held is more or less horizontal (and that unfortunately is not the best position for you to read the information on the set's LCD display) and the VOR range is limited to about 25 miles. Both the communications and the navigation range of a hand-held can be improved greatly if it is connected to an external aerial; the foregoing figures refer to its use only with its own antenna.

Keep it Safe

If you do decide to treat yourself to one of these transceivers, please try not to let it get stolen. That is not just because its disappearance might be inconvenient and because if it wasn't insured it would mean you had lost a few hundred pounds worth of equipment. Several of these transceivers seem to have fallen into the wrong hands and some idiots have tried to use them to make spurious pseudo ATC transmissions in attempts to mislead pilots. Fortunately, once the batteries run out the culprits usually don't have any means of recharging them, so the nuisance transmissions cease. I am pretty sure too, that once you have found out what an advantage it is for you to have a hand-held transceiver, you certainly wouldn't want to lose it, even if only for selfish but practical personal reasons.

Electronic Calculators etc.

During your flying training days you will initially have been bamboozled by (but hopefully will have eventually come to learn and love) what is still known as a 'flight computer'. It does seem rather odd nowadays, with all these PCs and laptops around, still to call this archaic looking metal or plastic gadget, with no monitor screen, no keyboard and no electrical power, a 'computer'. That is perhaps one reason you quite often hear it referred to as a 'whiz-wheel' or even as a 'Dalton' (after the inventor of the original model). Despite its outwardly complicated appearance, the old whiz-wheel turns out to be fairly simple to use, provided you remember the few simple basic rules. It has a lot more than that going for it too, as it never runs out of battery power, has virtually nothing in it that can go wrong and it produces results that are quite accurate enough for any private pilot's navigational purposes. Despite all these significant advantages that the whiz-wheel has over its modern electronic counterparts, more and more pilots are now using the new battery powered rivals of the old flight computer. These are actually little more than specialised electronic calculators, which allow pilots to dispense with all the business of sliding pieces of plastic across each other, aligning circular scales and cursers, peering at closely spaced graduation markings on the conversions scales, and calculating triangles of velocities by putting pencil marks on translucent plastic. They seem more familiar to fingers that have become accustomed to pressing buttons to get cash out of bank auto-teller machines, keying information into PCs and working with press-button radio selectors and GPS receivers. If you have really mastered the traditional (or old-fashioned?) type of flight computer you may well be of the opinion that real pilots don't use these battery powered toys, and you will soldier on with your good old plastic E6B, ARC-1, CRP-5 or whatever, and never miss the newfangled equivalents. But if you are more accustomed to handling PCs, mobile phones, ATMs and things of that sort, you will probably feel much more comfortable after you switch to one of the electronic variety.

Come to think of it, when did you last see a design engineer using a conventional slide rule?

Like their metal or plastic forebears, these gadgets will work out virtually any aviation conversion; nautical miles, statute miles, kilometres; fahrenheit/centigrade; gallons/litres; pounds/kilograms etc, and they do so at the touch of a couple of buttons and then display the results clearly and unmistakably on a liquid crystal screen display. They also solve triangles of velocities and work out headwind and crosswind components, as well as headings and groundspeeds, without using sliding scales and chinagraph pencil marks. In addition to performing all the calculations that the old whiz-wheel will do, the electronic ones can also act as timers, will calculate your aircraft centre of gravity and warn you when it is time to switch from one fuel tank to another.They can also be used for any non aviation mathematical calculation you might want to work out. Pricewise, the electronic versions are rather dearer than the equivalent mechanical ones, but the price ranges tend to overlap, with low-cost electronics being less expensive than top of the range mechanical slide rule ones. They run on standard dry-cell batteries which last for many hours of use (but are of course always liable to let you down at the most awkward time) and are slim enough to fit into a shirt pocket. Like their forerunners they all take a bit of getting used to, but once you become familiar with the electronic programs and how to use them, your old flight computer is liable to start gathering dust.

Microchip Checklists

Similar in general appearance, but designed for a totally different purpose, are electronic checklists. These require a special data cartridge, for whichever aircraft you are flying, to be inserted and once this is done they prompt you through the correct sequence for all the checklists used on that type of aircraft. Preflight, pre-start, emergency, downwind etc, are all there and data cartridges are available for a wide variety of light aircraft. Each item appears on the unit's LCD screen and remains on display until you carry out the check and press a button to tell it that you have effected the check. It is an excellent way in which pilots who have less than perfect memories, can ensure that they don't omit items from their vital actions, and it is, perhaps, slightly less easy to forget something when using one of these than when your eye or your finger skips past one of the items on a printed checklist.

Portable Flight Planners

Much more sophisticated in nature and in programming than the electronic checklists, are the navigation and flight planning programs which have been written to run on hand-held organisers (computers) such as the Psion. Leaving the enormous versatility of the basic organiser still fully available, the flight planning programs consist of databases which contain an enormous volume of aviation facts and figures. For example, for each of the hundreds of aerodromes in the database the precise latitude/longitude position is stored, together with such things as: ICAO code; all VHF frequencies; phone numbers; runway directions, lengths and surface type; altitude; lighting; types of instrument approach; ILS frequencies and idents, etc. Naturally, since they are based on much more powerful electronic circuitry than the electronic calculators described above, these organiser units also take easily within their stride the computation of track, heading, groundspeed and time, and can do all the relevant conversions, including IAS/RAS/TAS etc. It is often possible to programme in details of the aircraft you fly, and this enables the organiser to work out for you the fuel you are going to burn, flight costs, weight and balance calculations. Many of them can even give worldwide sunrise and sunset times. Some databases of this type are designed more for IFR than VFR operations, and these include all airways, MSAs, SIDs, STARs and so on; others have been programmed primarily with VFR flyers in mind. It is as well not to get involved with a program that is any more complicated (and more expensive to maintain up to date) than you really require. Certain versions of this type of organiser program come ready to be coupled to a GPS receiver. These have the capacity to display on the organiser screen a miniature moving map based on all the navigation data contained in the basic database.

Private Met Office
Another piece of electronic gadgetry that appeals to some pilots is known as a home weather station. This, once you have installed it, complete with its ancillary anemometer and other sensors, enables you to read from its LCD screen the wind speed and direction, ambient temperature, wind chill factor, barometric pressure and even the present time and date, all at the touch of a button or two. You can, if you wish, connect the weather station to a PC and it will then summarise and store all the collected data for graphing, and recall at will. This could be a fascinating gizmo for the pilot with other reasons beyond flying for being interested in the weather, but I don't see many private pilots choosing to use a home weather station as a substitute for TAFs, METARs and synoptic charts for their preflight briefings.

GPS Navigators

The methods by which aircraft have been navigated through the skies have evolved steadily throughout powered flight's 100 year history. Map reading and dead-reckoning were complemented by astro-navigation, then simple radio beacons and airborne loop aerials brought a new accuracy to navigation when the surface was obscured. Radar in all its various forms, directional radio beams, VHF omni-directional beacons and instrument landing systems were all developed over the years to improve navigational accuracy and increase safety. The latest, and possibly the largest, single step in aerial navigation technology came during the 1990s. This was the launch by the USA of their Navstar satellites to provide the basis for their Global Positioning System (GPS). Almost simultaneously the then Soviet Union launched another constellation of satellites which now is maintained and operated by Russia and serves their Global Navigation Satellite System (GLONASS). The principles of these satellite systems are too complex to describe in detail here and sufficient magazine articles and text books on the subject already exist to satisfy the interested reader. Suffice it to say that GPS (with or without GLONASS) has the potential to offer pilots a navigation system of hitherto unmatched accuracy. It is possible that future developments may extend this usefulness into the field of instrument landing but this, at the time of writing, is a prospect that is fraught with uncertainties, some technological, some political.

It is my opinion that satellite navigation will inevitably become an accepted and fully approved method of navigation, at least for light aircraft operated by the private pilot readers of this book. At the time of writing it is permitted as a primary or back-up method of navigation, to a greater or smaller extent by different national aviation authorities. Nothing contained in this section should be taken as implying that a pilot does have authority to navigate within the airspace of any particular state either solely, or partly, by reference to satellite derived data. You must always check the current legal situation for yourself as this is constantly changing territory.

The signals sent out by satellite systems require special receivers to put them to use and a wide and growing selection of these has burgeoned onto the aviation market since the GPS first became operational. The price of a basic receiver has tumbled since the early days of GPS, and some relatively low-cost receivers designed for aviation purposes now incorporate many sophisticated and useful special functions. Other non-aviation GPS receivers exist too, designed for use by yachtsmen, mountaineers, car drivers etc and, although some of these are priced at a mere fraction of the cheapest aviation versions, they do not offer all the facilities that are needed by a pilot user and which make GPS such a versatile light aircraft navigation system. The Global Positioning System has the ability to pinpoint your position anywhere around the world to within a few metres. For security purposes the Americans built in to GPS an ability to apply a selective degradation of this accuracy for civilian users, but agreement has been reached that this practice will shortly be discontinued. Thus, in future, both military and civilian pilots will be able to enjoy all the benefits of the system's extremely high precision.

Aviation GPS receivers come in a wide and constantly increasing variety of specifications. The simplest of the stand-alone units will provide a screen display of latitude and longitude (and height, though this last is generally less precise than the latitude and longitude) and have a database which you can load yourself with all the way points you wish to use; aerodromes, turning points, towns, navaids or anything else you choose to enter. The typical aviation GPS receiver has an array of buttons to press which will enable you to enter and memorise a route using whichever of these way points you need, or instantly to give you heading and distance to 'go to' any of them directly. It will display your course, track, groundspeed, time en route, estimated time of arrival and many other bits of navigational information, depending on the design of receiver and the way you program it. More complex GPS units have the ability to accept professionally compiled database cartridges, such as the Jeppesen ones which include an enormous fund of aviation information about each aerodrome and its facilities, each navaid, reporting point and so on, over vast areas of the earth's surface. To keep these accurate and up-to-date it is necessary to change them regularly and a service to do this is available, albeit at a cost. It is highly desirable for any flyer, including VFR pilots, to update these databases frequently and this is absolutely essential for IFR operations.

Moving Maps
Almost all GPS sets have an output connection which enables them to feed positional data into another unit that can display a moving map. Even more convenient are the many units now on the avionics market that incorporate the GPS receiver, the moving map and data display screen all in one unit. This map display can be a relatively crude sketch map of the area being overflown showing, in white lines on a black or green background, the approximate line of the coast and the positions of airfields, navaids and large towns. It can be made a little more detailed, to include airspace boundaries and other relevant aviation data, or it can display much greater detail right up to showing a full colour representation of an ICAO half-million aeronautical chart.

145

All this detailed information is derived from databank cartridges and, like the databanks referred to above, the information used to make these moving maps appear on screen must be maintained up to date if you want them to remain useful and safe for you to navigate by. Some GPS receivers have been designed specifically for use with laptop or other PCs in the cockpit, providing the PC with positional information, which it then displays on screen along with the moving map data extracted from its integral database.

It has to be admitted that there are limitations to the usefulness and reliability of GPS, but these drawbacks are reducing all the time. As is the case with VORs, NDBs, VHF radios and virtually all navigation aids, there remains a small possibility of the Global Positioning System breaking down, being jammed, or otherwise interfered with, so it cannot implicitly be relied upon for navigation under all circumstances. Keeping your eye firmly on where you are, on an old-fashioned paper chart, is a good insurance policy against finding yourself being let down unexpectedly by these mystic signals from inner space. That said, you will most probably find that if you do invest in a GPS moving map system, you will get continuous and reliable information from it each and every time you use it.

A GPS moving map makes accurate navigation childishly simple. That, and the way in which you can so easily interpret GPS information, does sometimes have an unfortunate side effect that you should do your best to guard against. It can tempt the unwary VFR pilot into flying in weather conditions that are really beyond his or her flying ability. In poor visibility you do feel so much safer knowing exactly where you are, knowing for certain that you haven't drifted a few miles off course, closer than is healthy to controlled airspace, hills or a TV transmitter mast. But always bear in mind that your trusty GPS *could* let you down. Before you get carried away by technology and find yourself out of your depth, just take a moment to visualise how you would feel if that marvellous little map screen (or even the basic GPS receiver navigation data screen) suddenly went blank. Would you still feel so comfortable hurtling on through the clag then? If the honest answer to that question is in the negative, then you owe it to yourself and to your passengers to resist the temptation to press on. Don't let yourself be lulled into a false sense of security by these useful, but potentially evanescent, electronic lines on a little glass screen.

GPS receivers come in a wide variety of permutations. As mentioned, they are available with integral moving maps, and also as independent receivers you can couple to slave map units. Hand-held GPS receivers with or without maps, moving map programs to load onto laptop PCs, panel mounted GPS sets, and many other variations on these themes, also exist. Not all of these will be ideally suited to the type of flying you want to do, nor to the type of aircraft you use for most of your flying. The GPS that best suits an aircraft owner may not suit a pilot who flies aircraft hired from flying clubs. A laptop PC-based moving map may be all right in a large cockpit, but very difficult to cope with in a cramped one. You may be prepared to accept a spider's web of wires connecting GPS, cigar lighter, antenna and display unit, but other pilots would loathe flying with that kind of tangle of cables in the cockpit. It pays to check the current catalogues carefully, and to make sure you haven't missed something that would more perfectly dovetail in with your particular requirements and your budget. Manufacturers are coming out with new and improved designs all the time in this fast moving and exciting branch of avionics.

PC Flight Simulators

It is getting close to the stage where one could claim that no pilot's kit is complete without a Personal Computer. Either sitting on a desk, or as a laptop in the cockpit, these gadgets are becoming, admittedly not quite indispensable, but certainly extremely useful tools (and toys) for pilots. Personal computers can do much more than run boring old accounts programs, produce spreadsheets, help designers with CAD programs, operate as word processors and keep the kids happy with endless games. They can keep many pilots quietly contented for hours too with flight simulator programs. All that you need to join in (apart from the PC and the programs themselves) is a games card in the PC, and preferably a pseudo aircraft control system with a joystick or yoke, and perhaps rudder pedals as well, plugged into the PC games card.

Flight simulator programs fall into several classes. One class essentially comprises all the many games flight simulator programs, involving high-power contemporary or futuristic jet fighters, World War II aircraft or even flimsy World War I planes, in various battle situations. These are much more suited to entertaining children (of all ages) than they are to educating pilots. Another class of program can be much more interesting to pilots and would-be pilots. This is the type of simulator with lots of realistic scenery on screen. These programs often have a wide range of aircraft, from microlights to Boeing 747s, any of which you can select as the one you want to 'fly'. Best known amongst these programs are probably *Microsoft's Flight Simulator, versions FS4 and FS5*. A huge library of scenery from all parts of the world has now been built up for these, some by Microsoft and some by other programmers. As well as comprehensively covering its homeland of the USA, this program scenery now enables PC pilots to fly, in simulation, into and out of any airport in Europe as well as many of the smaller airfields and airstrips on this side of the Atlantic. FS4 and FS5 were not really designed as flying training tools but they can, and do, enable pilots of real aeroplanes to learn quite a lot about cross-country navigation plus the airfield layouts and local area landmarks around places they have never previously visited. Certain procedural training can also be done with this type of program. A great deal of fun can be had from them too, enabling inexperienced Cessna pilots to learn at least something about, for example, the different handling characteristics of aerobatic aircraft perhaps, or light twins or even airliners. They are totally unrealistic in many ways (you can bring a Boeing in to land on a short grass strip if you wish and you appear to encounter no untoward problems). With many programs you can even happily fly unscathed through mountains or buildings, which is not a habit real pilots can survive. Yet in other ways these programs can be remarkably realistic. There are many pilots who get endless pleasure out of their simulator flying as well as their actual time in the air. The simulated flying also has the huge advantage that it comes virtually free of charge once the PC and programs have been bought.

A similar competitive flight simulator program written specially to simulate heavier aircraft is *SubLOGIC's Flight Assignment ATP (Airline Transport Pilot)*. Here the armchair pilot can select from a range of jet airliners; Boeing 737, 767 or 747, Airbus A-320 or a Shorts 360 turbo-prop, and fly the chosen machine through adjustable weather and scenery to land at any of over 900 instrument landing equipped US airports. With the right PC equipment you can even arrange to hear the voices of the ATC controllers giving instructions as you fly.

Learning Tools

Other flight simulator programs for PCs are designed specifically for flying training rather than largely for entertainment. Many require high specification computers to work correctly, others involve the purchase of more ancillary equipment than the usual control yoke (or joystick) and rudder pedals. In some cases you need to invest in a control console with throttle, flap and undercarriage levers and simulated engine controls. Some simulators of this type have gained FAA approval in the States and time spent at their controls may be logged as simulated instrument flying. These can be configured to represent various specific types of aircraft and their software is fully capable of faithfully replicating the performance of these types of aircraft. Programs of this advanced type include *Elite, On Top, Instrument Pilot* and *JetStream 300,* whilst *IFT Pro* is typical of the slightly less sophisticated IFR training simulators which are still very realistic but considerably less expensive. Less demanding on the PC hardware required, but still giving very useful experience in how to fly on instruments with reference to navaids, are inexpensive simulator programs like the *Radio Aids Navigation Tutor* by Oddsoft, *Flying Blind* by Freddie Nicholls (an 'add-on' to FS4 or FS5) and *MicroNav* by RC Simulation.

The pilot who has access to a PC (preferably an industry-standard IBM-compatible with at least a 386 processor) is certainly in a position to polish up many navigation and instrument flying skills before expensive time actually spent in the air. Instrument qualified pilots can also use programs of this type to keep these skills in practice. Even the private pilot with no immediate intention of going on to obtain an IMC or Instrument Rating, could get a great deal of fun out of FS4 or FS5. When the weather has clamped (or the finances have run dry for the month) and real VFR flying is out of the question, sometimes simulated VFR on a home computer is better than nothing. And a keen pilot can also pick up quite a lot of valuable information on how to make the best use of navaids, even in VFR, by using some of the other PC programs described here.

PC Logbooks, Flight Planners etc.

There are many other aviation programs on the market that have been written specifically for the private flyer. Some can even be downloaded free of charge or as 'shareware' from the Internet. If you have a personal computer and fancy backing up the bound copy of your flying logbook with an electronic version, you will find many programs for this purpose on the Internet. There are many more which cost money but are probably more sophisticated, and more thoroughly debugged, available for sale through pilot shops and the usual aviation mail order outlets. Most of these logbook programs have the advantage that they let you quickly and easily produce all sorts of specialised data from your log. Once you have flown a few hundred hours in a selection of different aircraft types, things like the number of hours solo time you have logged at night in Cessna 152, can take a lot of searching through pages of written entries. Any PC logbook program worth its salt should be able to give you that sort of information in a flash, as well as fun things like the number of times you have flown with a certain instructor, landed at a given airfield or even list the names of all the airfields you have ever landed at.

Educational PC programs on various aviation subjects are also prolific. There are simple ones to teach you the Morse Code, somewhat more complex ones to help you master instrument flying procedures, such as an ADF/RBI Tutor which covers things like NDB holds, track interception, coping with wind and drift, and a VOR Tutor which deals with both OBI and HSI presentations and covers all the IF applications of flying with reference to a VOR. You can run through programs such as these over and over again in front of your PC until the procedures are engrained into your mind. As a consequence, the time taken to pilot yourself through these procedures in the air should be much reduced . . . and the cost of your instrument qualification likewise.

For pilots who still haven't fully grasped the hows and whys of their Flight Computer there is a useful *Navigation Tutorial* training program from Griffon Aviation Software, which takes you through the procedure for whichever whiz-wheel you want to use and then persistently quizzes you about how to work its various functions, until you know you have grasped them all. The same company also publishes a PC program called the *PPL Training Kit*. Since most readers of this book probably have their PPLs already, I suppose I can only recommend this for revision purposes, or as a present for a PC-buff friend of yours who is thinking about learning to fly and might like an easily assimilated, highly graphical, version of the full PPL course to work through with keyboard, mouse and monitor.

The number of different ways you can use PCs in connection with private flying seems to grow steadily. Amongst the programs which I have found over the years to be most useful, are those written to help you with flight planning. None of these are particularly demanding on PC specification, many work in DOS, others in Windows, and some are available in both systems. In principle they are all similar. Each contains a database of aerodrome, navaid and other way point information, which must of course be kept up to date to guarantee safe and accurate flight plans. Each also contains software that quickly and precisely calculates distances and tracks, allows for wind, climb, descent and other factors, to produce times, groundspeeds, ETAs etc. Some will produce print-outs, not only of the flight log (which can even be run off in an ATC acceptable ICAO format) but of GPS coordinates, latitudes and longitudes of all way points, frequencies of all VHF stations you might want to use en route, and similar essential or highly desirable information. Even a long and complicated route, which would take for ever to plan in the conventional way with scales, protractors, charts and chinagraph pencils, can be produced in a few seconds by one of these number-crunching programs. Many PC flight planning programs have appeared on the market only to disappear again after a few months, but one which has, for very good reasons, stood the test of time is *Navtor*. This is available in several different forms, some of which can interface with a GPS, and each of which serves its particular purpose very competently. Other similar purpose programs include *Chocks Away*, *VFR Flight Planner for Windows* by Fast Technology, JENSoft's *Flight Manager of Windows* and MentorPlus's *FliteStar (Europe)*. Simpler programs with databases which you are required to fill and maintain by yourself, are also available. Some of these are free of charge on aviation sections of the Internet, just waiting for you to download and use them.

Details of most of the items mentioned in this chapter (and of a multitude of other pilots' playthings) are available from pilot shops and aviation supplies catalogues such as Pooley's, Transair Pilot Shop, JetStream Catalogue, Sporty's Pilot Shop Europa, PFA Pilot Shop etc.

Chapter 8

The Pilot's Ultimate Plaything

When is Your Own Aeroplane Worthwhile?

There cannot be many people who hold a Private Pilot Licence who have not at least thought about owning their own aeroplane, and those few pilots who do fall into that category almost certainly are going to start dreaming about it one day. Most of us never get beyond the stage of longing and wistfully dreaming about it, but quite a few hundred pilots in the UK, and many thousands world wide, do in fact own their own aeroplanes. Very frequently private aircraft ownership is a perfect example of the heart ruling the head. An elementary exercise in accountancy would prove that many owners would be a great deal better off if they simply contented themselves with flying aircraft they rented from a local club. Fortunately for flyers, accountants don't yet rule the world because there are many factors associated with aircraft ownership that just cannot be reduced to simple hard cash terms.

The convenience of having an aeroplane available as and when you want to fly, without having to book ahead or wait for ages at the club for one to come free for half an hour, is valuable to some. The fact that you can take your own machine away for the day, or the weekend, or for half a year should that happen to be what you want, without anyone muttering about minimum flying hours requirements, appeals greatly to others. Knowing how the aircraft has been treated at all times, being able to keep your own headsets, life-jackets, charts and other gear in it, never finding someone else's chocolate wrappers or cigar butts there when you open it up are all plus points for many owner pilots. Familiarity with all your own machine's quirks, how the radios and avionics work, where the control lock and sick bags are stowed, how much oil and fuel it burns, make flying your own aircraft much easier and more pleasurable than switching from one rented machine to another. It is impossible to measure any of these things in strictly financial terms. That is perhaps just as well, since without consciously, or subconsciously, using these unquantifiables to counterbalance the hard facts of financial calculations, not many private pilots would ever become aircraft owners.

The cost of aircraft ownership can be calculated in many ways, some more honest than others. You can look at the results either as an annual cost of ownership or, to make a comparison with renting, as a cost per flying hour. Paradoxically, it is necessary for you to spend more in total on your flying if you want to reduce the actual hourly cost. The reason is that, once you take the plunge into ownership, you are saddled with costs that must be borne whether or not you fly the thing at all. These include items like hangar (or tie-down) charges, insurance, depreciation and the annual inspection and C of A (or permit to fly) renewal. These so-called 'fixed' costs do actually vary enormously depending on where your base is, what type of aircraft you purchase, whether you do some of the maintenance work yourself and whether your pride and joy lives under cover or in the open air. For the sake of argument, taking these costs as a hypothetical figure of £5,000 per annum for a four seat 180 hp single, and assuming you were to fly it for no more than 40 hours during an average year, the fixed costs alone would amount to £125 per flying hour, before you start to look at the direct costs; the fuel and oil, building up a reserve for engine replacement, 50 hour checks, landing charges etc, which could very easily bring your hourly rate up to around £175. That makes the club aircraft look like a terrific bargain. It also shows why, if you don't intend logging many hours each year, you should very carefully weigh up how highly you personally value all these unquantifiable advantages of ownership, before you decide to buy.

On the other hand, once you own your own plane, you will almost certainly be encouraged to do more flying than you would do in rented aircraft. After all, you reckon, you are then paying all these fixed costs anyway, so the only extra expenditure an hour in the air is going to cost you, are the direct costs. If (as often) your hangar/tie-down rent includes local landings, these costs could be as little as £20 to £25 for an hour of local flying in a light aircraft. If you then fly 150 hours a year, instead of the 40 suggested above, the fixed cost element shrinks from £125 to around £35 per flying hour, and now you are beginning to be significantly in pocket, compared with renting a similar aircraft. In addition, you still have all the other advantages of ownership thrown in free of charge. There is no way I can suggest where the breakpoint in annual flying hours is likely to lie in your own case. There are just too many variables involved. But these hypothetical figures at least show that it is well worth your while doing some serious sums. Don't just jot down some figures on the back of an envelope, and let them convince you it is time you started seriously scrutinising the Aircraft

For Sale advertisements at the back of *Pilot* Magazine. Be absolutely sure that you can afford to keep your winged mistress, before you commit yourself to any purchase. There aren't many things that take the joy out of flying quite so effectively, as a growing pile of final demand statements that you can't afford to pay.

Aim a Little Lower

If the first set of calculations you do appears to show that you cannot justify that aeroplane of your own on which you have set your heart, there still may be a way round the problem. Many drivers setting out to buy their first car do rather fancy the idea of a high-power, high performance luxury sports coupe with all possible bolt-on goodies already bolted on. They end up, none the less, with a second-hand ex-salesman's 1300cc bog-standard saloon. Perhaps you should set your sights on something other that your ideal flying machine; something less exotic and less expensive so that it might suit your budget a little better. That could make a big difference to insurance costs as well as fuel and amortisation. It might also be worth considering keeping your aircraft at a different airfield, perhaps a little farther to drive to, but saving money on hangarage, tie-downs, landings and maybe even fuel. If however, your estimated utilisation of your own aeroplane is less than 100 hours, a year it is extremely unlikely that, however you juggle the figures, you will ever be able to justify it on an accountancy basis. You must then just decide for yourself how much extra you are willing to pay for the advantages that aircraft ownership brings.

How to Pick the Right Aeroplane

The Concise Oxford Dictionary defines an aeroplane as a mechanically-driven heavier-than-air flying machine. In the context of buying one for your own use a far better definition is that an aeroplane is a series of incompatible compromises. You have to trade a comfortable cabin against lower speed; a stable cruise against sluggish handling; size against cost; fuel efficiency against speed and so on. There isn't such a thing as a perfect aeroplane. The trick in aircraft buying is to pick an aeroplane whose design compromises *least* in the areas that matter *most* to you.

The world is full of people who seem to select the cars they buy because one of their main aims is to keep up with the Joneses. You can use this principle when you are looking for an aeroplane too, but believe me, it isn't the best way to pick a plane that suits you. If you don't get a real buzz from the look of little aeroplanes, if you don't find yourself feeling at least a little emotional about them, then you had better forget the whole idea of being an owner. Just keep on renting for those occasional flights you want to pilot and otherwise use your car or an airliner for your longer trips. If aeroplanes do turn you on and you really have the urge to own one, you must still try not to let emotion play too big a part in the selection process. You have to feel good about a plane when you see it; to feel that you are really going to enjoy sharing the skies with it, not just for today or next month, but probably for next year and a good few years longer than that too. Is it the right machine for the sort of flying you want to do? Enough space for the family, enough range to get to where you like going? Even if you lust after a high horsepower mean machine, be practical and remember how often you really need to get in and out of short grass strips to do the things you really enjoy doing. If your dream is of grass fields, blue skies and pottering quietly along enjoying the view below you, don't forget that if you make more than the occasional long flight (on business perhaps) there just might be a slight incompatibility somewhere around there. When you are sizing up your prospective purchase ask all these practical questions, but don't forget that the most important question of all probably is . . . does it look like it's going to be fun?

Decision Time

One of the first choices to be made is whether you want a single or a twin. The pros and cons of twins were discussed in Chapter 6. If money is no object, if you expect to have to fly in icing conditions and do a lot of your aviating over the sea or mountains then a twin just might make sense. But don't purchase one just for prestige. Remember that, statistically, you have twice the chance of experiencing engine failure in a twin and that anyone less than an experienced and proficient multi-engine pilot has less chance of surviving a single engine failure in a twin, than most pilots have of surviving after losing their only engine in a single.

I am therefore assuming that for the majority of readers the decision here will be quite decisively in favour of a single engine aeroplane. Then which single is the right one for your particular needs and wants? The answer to this is often contained in the prospective purchaser's bank book. What you would want in an ideal world and what is possible in practice, are often two entirely different things. But having determined where your financial limit lies, you may well find that it is still difficult to know what that will buy. In America various publications give guide prices for aircraft but in most European countries, the UK included, the market is too small for that to take place. The classified ads in the appropriate flying magazines give a general guide, although advertisers there often seem to have somewhat optimistic ideas of what their aeroplanes are really worth. A bit of old-fashioned negotiation (or haggling) frequently pays the purchaser handsomely. Similar sounding aeroplanes change hands at fairly widely varying prices too, depending on such things as whether they have any damage history, the engine life remaining, the state of interior furnishings and exterior paintwork, the value of the avionics fit and the age of the airframe. The American publications mentioned above can be useful reading for anyone contemplating following the oft-trodden path to the States to buy their aircraft there. *The Aircraft Bluebook Digest, The A/C Flyer, Vref* and *The Aircraft Bulletin* are useful sources of American used aircraft price information. There are also many pages of similar information available to download from the Internet.

Thus, even when you know exactly how much money you have available (or can persuade someone to lend you) there is still a great deal of choosing and deciding to do. It is easier on the whole to buy from someone in the country where you live, but there are times when currency fluctuations seem to make importing an aircraft a very attractive financial proposition. The base price you pay for the aircraft then is, however, only the beginning. You must bear in mind that shipping or flying your new toy to the UK, and then having it prepared for acceptance onto the CAA's UK register, can be expensive exercises to carry out. Then who do you buy from? An agent, a broker or a private individual? Each has its advantages; each has its drawbacks. Again we are back to weighing these up from the individual's point of view and choosing what is best under your own particular circumstances.

We now come to the choice of aeroplane. What about size for a start? Not many pilots really need a six-seat aircraft. Even if you do occasionally carry five passengers, the difference in running costs between a four and a six-seat machine will probably be enough to pay for the rent of a six-seater on the odd occasions you actually require one. In the other direction you may be mulling over the idea of a single seat aircraft for overall economy. Undoubtedly most of these are very much cheaper to buy and fly than two or four-seat aircraft, but is that really the only consideration for you? One seat is very limiting. You can fly solo in a two-seat aircraft but you can't take a passenger in a single seater, and flying does sometimes tend to get lonesome when every flight is another enforced solo.

High wing or low wing is generally a matter of personal choice. If Piper trained, you will probably have a predilection for low wing aircraft; Cessna trained pilots have a tendency to go in the other direction. There are technical arguments about high wing aircraft being more stable because their C of G is below the centre of lift and therefore gives a better ride in turbulence; they also give everyone a better view of the ground, at least until you as pilot really need a good view while you bank as you are approaching to land. Personal preferences and prejudices play a bigger part here than any aerodynamic theories; until they start building Boeing Jumbos and supersonic attack aircraft with their wings above their pilots' heads I personally shall continue to content myself with low wing aeroplanes.

Another question to which there is no clear-cut technical answer is whether you should buy a metal aeroplane or a wooden one, or even come right bang up to date and become the proud owner of a sexy, curvaceous aircraft made by bonding together foam cores, pre-preg glass fibre and carbon fibre composite materials. Each has its advantages and disadvantages. If that were not so you would not be likely to find aeronautical engineers still arguing over their relative merits and still designing new aircraft for production in each of these three materials. There is no doubt though, that the vast majority of the second-hand machines you will have to choose from will turn out to be of metal construction, so the probability is that, unless you make a determined effort to go for one of the other materials, it is a metal aeroplane that you will end up owning.

If you intend doing a great deal of your flying at high altitude, a turbocharged aircraft might be worth considering. Otherwise you would be better to leave these designs strictly alone. For the majority of owners the extra fuel which turbocharged aircraft burn, and the extra maintenance costs they bring, can negate any speed and climb advantages they might have. Likewise, unless you are one of these people who just has to be different, steer clear of anything too exotic. Some unusual aircraft are difficult to insure for a start. Some may be fine until you need a spare and find that parts just don't exist any more. If you are not a knacky DIY person, but despite that still take a chance and buy someone else's home-built aircraft, you may find it very tricky to find any mechanics willing to maintain it for you.

Make a sensible analysis of what you want your aeroplane to do for you. Consider the type of flying you are most likely to be doing, the loads you will want to carry and the minimum range you really require. Be realistic. There is little point in paying over the odds just to save a couple of refuelling stops on the one or two really long flights you expect to make in the course of your average year's flying. It is too easy to fall into the trap of buying, on impulse, something with lots of bells and whistles that you are seldom, or never, going to make use of. Match your aircraft to your sensible requirements and you can save yourself a lot of money.

It is obviously always a good idea to fly the actual aircraft before you commit yourself to buying it. Less obvious perhaps is the thought that, even before you reach the stage of test flying your prospective purchase, it is an even better idea to rent a similar model for one or two trips if you can. That way you and your partner and/or family can get a much better feel for how it is likely to match up to your and their requirements. If you have a strong inclination towards one particular type of aircraft it is often worth finding out whether there is an active owners' club. These organisations often publish useful newsletters giving hints and tips about problems other owners have encountered and how these can be overcome. The information coming from owners' clubs is often a lot more accurate and informative, especially concerning performance figures, than even the data published by manufacturers. These brochure figures are really a form of advertising, and usually refer to brand-new aircraft flown by super competent pilots under ideal conditions. So far as performance is concerned, there is little point either in trying to obtain your data from 'independent' sources like *Pilot* or *Flyer* magazine flight reports or *Jane's All the World's Aircraft* because, with very few exceptions, the figures in these too are usually derived from the manufacturers' own suspiciously optimistic publications.

The Microlight Alternative

In recent years another class of aircraft has appeared on the scene, just to make the prospective purchaser's decision that much harder. These are the microlights or, as they are referred to in many other countries, ultralights. Differing from the conventional light aircraft on which you learned to fly mainly in terms of size, weight and fuel capacity, they represent an opportunity of getting into ownership of a single or two-seat aircraft, for a significantly lower investment than a conventional two-seat aircraft. Microlights started off as little more than hang-gliders with power units, but they have developed a long way since then and some of the three-axis control microlights (these are the ones that look more or less like normal light aircraft) can be flown by anyone who holds a Group (A) PPL. It is advisable though, to have a microlight pilot at least check you out first, and it would probably be even better for you if you did a proper microlight conversion course. Some of these machines have special characteristics of their own which come as a bit of a surprise to pilots who have been accustomed to nothing other than a basic Piper or Cessna trainer. On the other hand, some microlights are almost indistinguishable in their handling from normal aircraft. Indeed some designs are available in two different versions, one classified as a microlight and another as a

Group A aeroplane. Many are also available in kit form for home building. The capital cost of a microlight can be much less than that of a normal aircraft, but the new price of some top-of-the-range microlights is appreciably more than you would need to pay for a reasonably good, even if well-used, conventional two-seat aircraft. It is in the running costs that microlights really score. They sip much less fuel, are less costly to maintain, can be hangared cheaply (often in a trailer or garage) and landing fees for them are generally very low. If your aircraft ownership ambitions are bigger than your financial means, it could certainly be worth making contact with the British Microlight Aircraft Association. They will put you right on all you need to know about this interesting and economical branch of private flying.

Check before Cheque

Unless you are technically qualified you should get an engineer you know and can trust to give your potential purchase a thorough inspection. This must include compression checking each cylinder, a corrosion (or glue joint) inspection, a cross-check of aircraft and component serial numbers (to make sure you aren't buying hot property) and a good read through the logbooks etc, to ensure no documents are missing and that there aren't any expensive Airworthiness Directives (AD) or service bulletins that haven't been complied with. Ideally, your friendly engineer should be pretty conversant with the type of aircraft you are buying. Almost any fault in an aeroplane can be put right, but skilled engineers' time doesn't come cheap, so if the machine you are considering has something wrong with it, make doubly sure that any estimated repair costs are realistic. Once the aircraft becomes your property, it is you who will have to pay these bills. Don't be misled though, by too dismal prognostications from your engineer about previous repairs; like dentists and hairdressers, many engineers just love to criticise other peoples' work.

Once you have finally decided on the aircraft of your dreams, do your utmost to make sure the owner has a clear title to it, free from any outstanding loans, co-owners, or other financial encumbrances. Then, after you have negotiated a mutually satisfactory price, arranged any necessary finance and agreed the date you take over the keys of your very own aeroplane, don't be in so much of a hurry to fly it away that you forget to arrange insurance cover. Even a minor mishap in the course of an uninsured delivery flight could quite spoil the start of your life as an aircraft owner.

Building your Own Aeroplane

The 'do-it-yourself' route into aircraft ownership is an attractive one from many points of view. There are many good looking and capable designs of aeroplane now available for home construction. The range of aircraft that can be self-built under PFA supervision, and flown on Permit, has been extended during the 1990s to include four-seaters and aircraft fitted with higher horsepower engines than formerly was allowed. This is a far cry from a few decades back when a home-built was nearly always a slow, low power contraption with an ugly boxy looking fuselage and a rectangular wing that looked as though it had been temporarily stuck on either above or below it.

Home building has a long and, on the whole, honourable history. The idea really got off the ground in France in the interwar years when Henri Mignet designed the *Pou du Ciel*, known as the 'Flying Flea' in English speaking countries (where the literal translation 'Louse of the Skies' doesn't have quite the right ring about it). A series of articles in *Practical Mechanics* described how the Flea could be flown by just about anyone, and detailed how it could be built in a garage using no more than a simple set of tools. The enthusiasm for this idea was the catalyst that brought the Ultra Light Aircraft Association (ULAA) into being in Britain. It had the blessing of the authorities to help enthusiasts to design and build their own aircraft. The *Pou du Ciel*, alas, was not the great success its designer had anticipated, but members of the ULAA did produce quite a few respectable little aircraft of other designs before World War II came along and put an abrupt end to their activities. In 1946 the ULAA came back to life again, albeit under its new name, the Popular Flying Association (PFA) and it is to the PFA that anyone in the United Kingdom wanting to build an aircraft of his or her own must turn. Those interested might also find it worth joining the American Experimental Aircraft Association (EAA) as well, to keep in touch with the tremendous strides in home building that have been made in recent years in the USA and to get their excellent newsletters. The PFA's own magazine *Popular Flying* is also a first-class publication for anyone intending to tackle the task of putting together an aircraft of his or her own.

The PFA can let members have details of all the kits that are approved for construction in the UK and has been designated by the CAA to oversee the design and construction, or restoration, of aircraft by private individuals. It is only by satisfying the quality requirements of the PFA's team of inspectors that anything you build yourself will be granted a Permit to Fly, without which it has to stay firmly on terra firma. So if you want to build your own aeroplane, then the earlier you contact the PFA the better are your chances of ultimate success. The PFA's Permit to Fly is the home-built aircraft's counterpart of the CAA's Certificate of Airworthiness for a commercially manufactured aircraft. It has, however, several limitations in comparison with a C of A, and these are worth considering carefully before you embark on this route to ownership. Permit aircraft are not allowed to fly over built up areas, except as necessary for landing and taking off. The Permit is not valid outside the UK, so any flights abroad will require prior clearance from the appropriate foreign authorities. (Normally this is just an inconvenient formality, as permission is usually freely granted.) You will not be permitted to fly at night, nor in IMC, and you are not allowed to use a Permit aircraft for any training, except the training of an owner or part-owner pilot.

Modern Designs and Materials

Home building has become less daunting for amateur aircraft engineers in recent years, with the introduction of modern construction materials and techniques such as Kevlar, carbon fibre, composite foam and glass fibre. These innovations have, to some extent at least, reduced the need for technical skills in tin-bashing or woodworking. Home-built aircraft have also gained considerably in reliability in recent years with the advent of better power units than the old converted Volkswagen flat-fours and McCullochs. The Rotax range of two and four-stroke engines in particular is proving very popular and reliable, whilst other home-built aircraft fly with a wide range of engines; Continental, Lycoming, Limbach, Subaru and new designs like the Zoche Diesel range, the Australian Jabiru, the rotary Wankels etc. Home building is not the preserve only of anorak clad tinkerers and cranks, nor is it restricted solely to expert craftsmen and women. That said, unless you are one of those people who really enjoy building things, the chances are rather slender of you making a successful entry into the world of home building. On the other hand, lack of experience is no bar; few people who start their own DIY aeroplane have ever built one before . . . though some gluttons for punishment are known to have actually built with their own hands, four or more. You will almost certainly have to be prepared to learn some new skills, but specialist aspects of the work such as welding, if required, are probably best left to experts. You might also experience a different sort of problem if you opt for one of the 'easier' designs that involve working with epoxy resins, glass fibre and bonding agents. You could find that you are one of those unfortunate people who are allergic to some of these things.

Why do People Do It?

Why would you want to build an aircraft of your own? Some people take this route so that they can have a design of aircraft that satisfies their requirements better than any production aeroplane they can find. Some because they feel they will get more machine for their money this way. Others simply because they want to enjoy the immense satisfaction of constructing something really worthwhile with their own hands, and then following that with the exhilarating feeling of actually taking to the air in something that they have just built.

Those in the third of these categories are the ones most likely to achieve their aim. Those in the first category might be lucky too. But the ones who get into home building mainly in order to save money are liable to be disappointed. A set of plans and the material needed to build an aeroplane to the required design, certainly come a whole lot cheaper than a completed aeroplane; that goes without saying. But to get the materials transmogrified into a flying machine takes endless hours of labour. Your own labour you may choose to disregard so far as cost is concerned, but outside labour and workshop space, light and heating, all have to be budgeted for. Making one tiny mistake with an expensive sheet of plywood or plastic or aluminium can put up the building costs too. Very few people construct aeroplanes direct from plans these days. They buy kits, and these invariably work out rather more expensive than basic raw materials. Kits do, of course, have the valuable attribute of being quite a lot quicker to turn into finished aeroplanes. All in all, the true finished cost of a self-built light aeroplane is likely to be appreciably more than the cost of a similar second-hand machine in fair to good condition. But no second-hand aircraft is ever going to give you the same rewards as that ultimate thrill of taking into the air something you lovingly created with your own hands.

It All Takes Time

Concerning build time, don't embark on this sort of project without thinking this factor through carefully. Most kit manufacturers quote a suggested build time for their kits. Most members of PFA will tell you that, as a first-time builder, you are going to find these times unattainable. If the kit claims that 'only' 1,000 man-hours are needed to construct it, take that with a pinch of salt. Call it at least 1,250 or perhaps closer to 1,500 hours. Ask other PFA members who have built the design in question and you'll get a better feel for the time that's actually involved. If it turns out to be 1,500 hours that may not sound much when you say it quickly, but it translates into a whole lot of your life. It means, for instance, that you work on your kit for two hours a day, every day, weekends included, for 750 days. So if you do your two hours per day religiously, then put in an extra few hours most weekends and don't take any holidays for the next two full calendar years, you should just about manage to complete it in that time. It takes dedication. It takes something else for married people too; an understanding, sympathetic and perhaps even helpful spouse. Are you sure she (or he) will accept wood shavings and glue smells in the kitchen, epoxy resin curing in the lounge, your absence, hour upon hour every evening, the noise of drilling or rivetting drowning the Mozart on the hi-fi or the television sound?

Changed Lifestyle

It is pretty obvious then, that building your own aeroplane the DIY way is going to make hefty inroads into the rest of your life. Something has to give; any other hobbies, certainly; much of your flying, probably. Evenings in front of the television or at the cinema will become rarities; the garden could turn into a wilderness, so far as you are concerned; what the rest of the world knows as DIY (that plebeian stuff around the house) will have to take a back seat. Are you and your partner (if any) really prepared to make that sort of sacrifice? If your honest answer is 'yes', then go ahead and good luck to you. You could be embarking on a project that will bring you more real satisfaction than any other hobby you could take up. People who have succeeded in getting their home-built aircraft completed and into the air will tell you (and everybody else in their vicinity) just what a feeling of achievement that brought them, and how amply it compensates for all the years of hard work and hardship that went before the flying. If, however, you frankly don't feel you are ready to make the sacrifices involved and to devote so much of your time to the project, then go back to the previous section of this Chapter and start looking for a ready-made machine. Just because you aren't prepared to dedicate the next two years or so of your life to sanding and sawing, bending metal or bonding mastic, there is no need to give up on all the thrills and joys of doing your flying in your very own aeroplane.

The Next Best Thing . . . Group Flying

You have added up the costs of building your own aeroplane and decided that either the time, the work or the money involved is more than you can afford. You have compared the prices of the production aircraft in *Pilot* and *Flyer* classified aircraft for sale adverts with your available cash and you have concluded, sadly, that purely for financial reasons you and aircraft ownership don't quite match. Fortunately there is another alternative before you have to give up at this stage. Don't decide just yet that you will just have to continue to book ahead to hire the old club Cessna, as and when you and it happens to be free at the same time.

Instead, you could join a group. You could even form one.

Group flying combines many of the advantages of private ownership with some of those of club flying. Unfortunately it also combines certain of the disadvantages of both. The traditional flying group is made up of a few pilots who have come together to share the flying of an aeroplane which none of them individually could afford to buy or operate. The pilots making up the group probably all fly mainly for fun, rather than for business, and each is prepared to pay his or her own share of the fixed costs involved. Each must also be willing to do something towards the chores involved in aircraft ownership, and to get together as partners and friends every so often to elect office bearers, transact group business, and generally enjoy each others' company.

Sharing an Interest
The principle of getting together with several other people to do group flying may perhaps seem just a little anachronistic. After all in today's world people are more accustomed to the beggar-your-neighbour attitudes of the rat race, to families who rarely even sit down to eat together and to general apathy towards many community activities. Despite that, in terms of making it possible to enjoy what is tantamount to private use of an aeroplane, for much less capital outlay and lower running costs, there is a great deal to be said in favour of groups; always assuming that the pilots involved get along well together and all contribute something more than just cash to the running of the group. Group flying can then quite adequately fill the awkward gap that yawns between the frustrations of renting from a club, and committing yourself to the expense of full ownership. A single owner often ends up by flying relatively little and so the utilisation of the aircraft is poor, leading to exorbitant hourly costs when all the amortisation, insurance and other fixed costs are considered. A few pilots could band together around that same aircraft, shove the utilisation up to say 400 hours per annum, and so bring down drastically the share of the fixed costs that each flying hour must bear. It also enables a group of like-minded pilots to fly something more interesting than the aeroplanes likely to be on offer from local flying clubs. Instead of a trainer or a typical club operated tourer, the group could fly an old-timer or an aerobatic machine if the pilots had a mind to, or a higher speed tourer like a

Bonanza or Mooney perhaps. Alternatively it could head for a lower performance, less expensive model to keep down fuel and overall operating costs.

A group will provide its members with regular access to a familiar cockpit. Club pilots have to fly whichever aircraft happens to be free in whatever condition the last user left it. As a member of a group, you will fly what is your own aeroplane (at least in part) and the others who also fly it are again part-owners. They will, you trust, also have a proprietorial interest equal to your own in keeping the machine in good condition. On the other hand group membership involves you in more than just walking up to the operations desk at the club and asking for the keys. You are expected to take on some of the chores of ownership, like helping to wash and wax the bird, keeping the engine and airframe logs up to date, organising the group activities (social and otherwise), keeping the books, collecting dues, writing and distributing group communications, paying the bills, ensuring that routine servicing and maintenance are done, etc.

Good Rules - Secrets of Success

If you join an established group or answer one of the advertisements in *Pilot, Popular Flying, Flyer* etc where someone is trying to form a group, you will have to accept, by and large, the existing rules and regulations. When it is you forming a new group with some fellow pilots, you have to devise a suitable format for your group. It can be a cost sharing group around one privately owned aircraft, where members contribute towards the overheads and pay a basic hourly rate for flying. Alternatively, each member may become a part-owner of the aircraft and each flies it paying the basic direct costs. There are various rather complicated CAA rules and insurance requirements that affect this decision, and these should be carefully considered before the group constitution is drawn up. The number of members is an important point too. Too few and the main objective of improving utilisation to reduce flying costs may not be achieved. Too many and you will be back to the problem of getting hold of the aircraft when you want it, especially if the members are all of the type who prefer to fly in the summer and then usually on Sunday afternoons. About five or six pilots is usually a good number; enough to cope with the various chores involved without anyone being overloaded with work, and not so many as to make scheduling the aircraft too difficult at busy times. If the majority of members are interested in flying long trips, four or five should be the maximum allowed to join. If most members fly, in the main, local pleasure trips only, then there should be room for a few more, especially if some of them are able to do their flying mid-week.

Membership dues should be invoiced each month to cover all the costs that tick relentlessly on whether a member flies or not. It is not a bad idea either to make it compulsory for each member to pay for one hour's flying with his or her monthly dues. That is forfeited to the group if the member doesn't fly that month. The idea behind this is to give an incentive to all members to maintain their proficiency, and if it fails in that aim, it at least compensates the group for the reduced utilisation of the aircraft.

When discussing the question of finance in Chapter 5, it was mentioned that there was one other set of circumstances, associated with group flying, in which a private pilot can legally accept payment in connection with his or her flying. This is in the case of a flight in a jointly owned aircraft; the payment involved must reflect the actual costs of the flight and must be made by one of the joint owners to another. Joint ownership in this case cannot involve more than twenty people and each joint owner must own at least a 5% share in the aircraft.

Choosing your fellow members is important. It isn't everyone who makes a good groupie and letting a wrong 'un in can have a distinctly adverse effect on everyone involved. If your group lacks a psychologist to vet all applicants, then at least get each would-be member to fill in a fairly thorough questionnaire with details of their flying experience, occupation, credit and personal references and what they would do with the group aircraft. It is well worth the trouble to try to run a credit check on the applicants. Some may object to this, but it is far better to lose a potential member at that stage than to end up with a problem member. It has been known for plausible types to turn up, join a group that doesn't do adequate checking, run up a bill for several hundred pounds worth of flying and then vanish without trace. The cost of their flying unfortunately doesn't vanish with them; it has to be borne by the remaining members. Some groups run into trouble if the rules allow any member leaving to sell his or her share directly to anybody else he or she chooses. It is safer to incorporate some clause making it compulsory to offer the share back to the group first, or at least to allow the other members to blackball anyone they regard as unsuitable. To make things run smoothly, each group needs officials to look after various jobs. A treasurer, a secretary and a safety officer are almost essential. General management, and looking after technical matters like maintenance of the aircraft, may be included in the duties of one or other of these, or may be allocated to another member or members.

Plane for all Members
Having got the group formed, or at least having established that sufficient suitable people are interested in the formation of a group, the

166

all-important next step is to select an aircraft to suit the needs of the membership and which is within the financial reach of the group. Is it to be used mainly locally or for longer trips? IFR or VFR? Does it need to be suitable for short strips? How many seats? Is cruising speed more important to members than fuel burn, or is it the other way round? Think long and hard over factors such as these, otherwise the group could get landed with what might well be a beautiful aeroplane, but one that is incompatible with the needs of the members. If that happens it doesn't get used enough and ultimately is liable to cause the group to fail. Another common cause of group troubles is financial problems, usually caused by under capitalization. Then there is always the danger of unanticipated unservicability of the group aircraft interrupting flying, and the cash flow it generates, and perhaps costing more to rectify than the group can afford to pay. For this reason it is sensible to try to build up some form of reserve, or contingency fund, in the group's bank balance and to insist that all members settle their accounts for flying promptly.

It does take quite a bit of work to organise and run a group operation successfully, but the rewards can be sweet. As a member of a non-profit-making organisation you should be able to fly for appreciably less cost than if you were still hiring from a commercially run school or club. You will certainly fly for significantly less than if you were sole owner of the same aeroplane. You are likely to build up close friendships with a number of people whose interests are similar to your own, and each one of you can enjoy having realised your cherished dream of owning an aeroplane, without needing to bear all the overhead expenses alone. If you are ready to surrender a little of your independence by going into partnership with some fellow pilots, you stand to gain a whole lot more than you lose.

Conclusion

Not many private pilots will ever manage to participate in more than a selection of the forms of flying suggested in the foregoing chapters. However, most PPL qualified pilots could derive a great deal of additional pleasure and satisfaction from their licences simply by trying to take part in each of the ideas that appeal to them.

It is only by branching out occasionally into new fields of flying that PPL holders can ever get full value from the investment made in obtaining their pilot qualification. All of us who have turned piloting into an important part of our lives started out with a dream of flight. Unlike the many who once had that dream in their heads but never had the belief that they could learn to fly, we belong to the few who took on the challenge and turned the dream of flight into reality. When we made it come alive we took our first steps along what has the potential to be a fascinating and rewarding journey.

If *Progressive Flying* helps to encourage some readers to investigate a few of aviation's avenues they would otherwise never have explored, it will have served its purpose. Its author has obtained a great deal of pleasure and satisfaction from piloting during the half century that has passed since his first flight. His aim in sharing these ideas, suggestions and experiences is to help readers to get as much enjoyment out of flying in all its varied aspects as he has been lucky enough to do.

Flying involves a mixture of emotions and events. Every pilot loves it at times and hates it at others. It is full of pitfalls and disappointments but these are more than compensated for by the delights, successes, excitement and exhilaration. There are occasional times in every pilot's life when he or she feels a bit like throwing in the towel. Whenever one of these times does come along, leave that towel where it is, dig out this book and find another challenge to tackle that will keep the beautiful dream alive.

ABBREVIATIONS

aal	Above Aerodrome Level
ADF	Automatic Direction Finding
agl	Above Ground Level
AIC	Aeronautical Information Circular
AIP	Aeronautical Information Publication (UK version also known as 'Air Pilot')
AIS	Aeronautical Information Service
amsl	Above Mean Sea Level
ANO	Air Navigation Order (UK)
AOA	Aerodrome Owners' Association
AOC	Air Operator's Certificate
AOPA	Aircraft Owners and Pilots' Association
ASI	Airspeed Indicator
ATC	Air Traffic Control
ATIS	Automatic Terminal Information Service
ATPL	Airline Transport Pilot's Licence
ATZ	Aerodrome Traffic Zone
BAeA	British Aerobatic Association
BWPA	British Women Pilots' Association
CAA	Civil Aviation Authority (United Kingdom)
CAD	Computer Aided Design
CAP	Civil Air Publication
CDI	Course Deviation Indicator
C of A	Certificate of Airworthiness
C of G	Centre of Gravity
CPL	Commercial Pilot's Licence
CTR	Control Zone
DAAIS	Danger Area Activity Information Service
DACS	Danger Area Crossing Service
DI	Directional Indicator or Gyro Compass
DME	Distance Measuring Equipment
EAA	Experimental Aircraft Association (USA)
EGT	Exhaust Gas Temperature (Gauge)
ETA	Estimated Time of Arrival
FAA	Federal Aviation Authority (USA)
FAI	*Fédération Aéronautique Internationale*
FBO	Fixed Base Operator
FCL	Flight Crew Licensing
FIR	Flight Information Region

FIS	Flight Information Service	METAR	Meteorological Aerodrome Report
FL	Flight Level	MHz	MegaHertz (10^6
FPL	Flight Plan		cycles/second)
FS4 & FS5	Versions of Microsoft Flight Simulator Program	MSA	Minimum Safe (or Sector) Altitude
		NDB	Non-Directional Radio Beacon
GA	General Aviation		
GFT	General Flight Test	NVQ	National Vocational Qualification
GLONASS	Global Navigation Satellite System (Russia)		
		OAT	Outside Air Temperature
GPS	Global Positioning System (USA)	OBI	Omni-bearing Indicator
HASELL	Vital actions before aerobatics etc:- Check Height, Airframe, Security, Engine, Location and Look-out	PC	Personal Computer
		PFA	Popular Flying Association
		POH	Pilot's Operating Handbook
		PPL	Private Pilot's Licence
HSI	Horizontal Situation Indicator	PPR	Prior Permission Required
IAS	Indicated Air Speed	QFE	Altimeter setting to give height above aerodrome
IAOPA	International Council of Aircraft Owners and Pilots Associations		
		QFI	Qualified Flying Instructor
ICAO	International Civil Aviation Organisation	QNH	Altimeter setting to give airfield elevation with aircraft on the ground
IF	Instrument Flight		
IFR	Instrument Flight Rules		
		RAeC	Royal Aero Club
IMC	Instrument Meteorological Conditions	RAS	Rectified Air Speed
		RAS	Radar Advisory Service
IR	Instrument Rating	RBI	Relative Bearing Indicator
JAA	Joint Airworthiness Authority (Europe)		
		RIS	Radar Information Service
JAR	Joint Airworthiness Requirements (Europe)		
		RT	Radiotelephony
		SID	Standard Instrument Departure
LARS	Lower Airspace Radar Service		
		SR	Sunrise
LCD	Liquid Crystal Display	SS	Sunset
MATZ	Military Aerodrome Traffic Zone	STAR	Standard Instrument Arrival

SVFR	Special Visual Flight Rules
SVQ	Scottish Vocational Qualification
TAF	Terminal Aerodrome Forecast
TAS	True Air Speed
TMA	Terminal Control Area
ULAA	Ultra Light Aircraft Association
VAT	Value Added Tax
VFR	Visual Flight Rules
VHF	Very High Frequency
VMC	Visual Meteorological Conditions
Volmet	VHF Met Report for aircraft in flight
VOR	VHF Omni-directional Range Radio Beacon
VRP	Visual Reporting Point
WW1/WW2	World Wars 1 & 2

USEFUL AVIATION ADDRESSES

Aerodrome Owners' Association
18 Orchard Street
BRISTOL
BS1 5DX
Tel: 01272-292480

Aeronautical Information Service
NATS, AIS Central Office
First Floor, Control Tower
Building
London Heathrow Airport
Hounslow, Middlesex
TW6 1JJ
Tel: 0181-745 3456

AFE Ltd
Southside
Manchester Airport
Wilmslow
Cheshire
SK9 4LL
Tel: 0161-499-0023
Fax: 0161-499-0298

AOPA (UK)
50a Cambridge Street
London
SW1V 4QQ
Tel: 0171-834 5631
Fax: 0171-834 8623

AOPA (USA) also for International
Partnership
421 Aviation Way
Frederick
Maryland MD 21701-9922
USA
Tel: (301) 695-2000
Fax: (301) 695-2375

Aviatours (Charter) Ltd
Pinewoods, Eglington Road
Tilford
Surrey
GU10 2DH
Tel: 01252-793250

British Aerobatic Association
White Waltham Airfield
Maidenhead
Berkshire
SL6 3NJ
Tel: 01455-617211

**British Microlight Aircraft
Association**
Bullring
Deddington
Oxfordshire
OX5 4TT
Tel: 018693-38888

British Precision Pilots' Association
Kenvale
Northview Avenue
Bideford
Devon
EX39 3LH

British Women Pilots' Association
Brooklands Museum
Weybridge
Surrey
KT13 0QN

Business Aircraft Users' Association
50 Rochester Row
London
SW10 1TU
Tel: 0171-828 6611

Civil Aviation Authority
CAA House
45-59 Kingsway
London
WC2B 6TE
Tel: 0171-379 7311

Civil Aviation Authority Flight Crew Licensing
Ground Floor, Aviation House
Gatwick Airport South
West Sussex
RH6 0YR
Tel: 01293-567171

Flyer Magazine
Third Floor
3 Kingsmead Square
Bath
BA1 2AB
Tel: 01225-481440
Fax: 01225-481262

Flying Farmers' Association
Ox House
Shobdon
Leominster
Herefordshire

HR6 9LT
Tel: 01568-708351

General Aviation Safety Committee (GASCO)
Church House
33 Church Street
Henley-on-Thames
Oxfordshire
RG9 1SE
Tel: 01491-574476

Jetstream Catalogue
Portland-Hillsboro Airport GAT Building
3355 N.E. Cornell Road
Hillsboro
Oregon OR 96124-6380
USA
Tel: (503) 693-3522
Fax: (503) 693-1822

Pilot Magazine
The Clock House
28 Old Town
Clapham
London
SW4 0LB
Tel: 0171-498-2506

Pooleys
Elstree Aerodrome
Elstree
Hertfordshire
WD6 3AW
Tel: 0181-207-3749
Fax: 0181-953-2512

Popular Flying Association
Terminal Building
Shoreham Airport
Shoreham-by-Sea
West Sussex
BN43 5FF
Tel: 01273-461616
Fax: 01273-463390

Royal Aero Club
Records, Racing and Rally
Association
Terminal Building
Shoreham Airport
Shoreham-by-Sea
West Sussex
BN43 5FF
Tel: 01273-461182

Service de l'Information Aéronautique
91205 Athis-Mons
CEDEX
France
Tel: 1-69 84 56 03/04
Fax: 1-69 84 56 02

Sporty's Pilot Shop (Europa) Inc
Hagenauer Str. 53
65203 Wiesbaden
Germany
Tel: 0611-22042
Fax: 0611-20898

Transair Pilot Shop
West Entrance Fairoaks Airport
Chobham
Woking
Surrey
GU24 8HU
Tel: 01276-858533
Fax: 01276-855464

Index